PERFORMANCE ASSESSMENT AND STANDARDS-BASED CURRICULA

THE ACHIEVEMENT CYCLE

Allan A. Glatthorn

with Don Bragaw, Karen Dawkins,
and John Parker

EYE ON EDUCATION
6 Depot Way West, Suite 106
Larchmont, N.Y. 10538

Library of Congress Cataloging-in-Publication Data

Glatthorn, Allan A., 1924-
    Performance assessment and standards-based curricula : the
achievement cycle / Allan A. Glatthorn with Don Bragaw ... [et al.].
        p.   cm.
    Includes bibliographical references.
    ISBN 1-883001-48-X
    1. Curriculum planning--United States.   2. Education--Curricula-
-Standards--United States.   3. Curriculum-based assessment--United
States.   4. Competency based education--United States.   5. Effective
teaching--United States.   I. Title.
LB2806.15.G5875   1998
374'.001--dc21   97-40094
                                                                      CIP

10 9 8 7 6 5 4

Editorial and production services provided by Richard H. Adin Freelance
Editorial Services, 9 Orchard Drive, Gardiner, NY 12525 (914-883-5884)

Published by Eye On Education:

The Performance Assessment Handbook
Volume 1: Portfolios and Socratic Seminars
by Bil Johnson

The Performance Assessment Handbook
Volume 2: Performances and Exhibitions
by Bil Johnson

Instruction and the Learning Environment
by James W. Keefe and Harry M. Crenshaw

A COLLECTION OF PERFORMANCE TASKS AND RUBRICS
Vol. 1: Middle School Mathematics
by Charlotte Danielson

Vol. 2: Upper Elementary School Mathematics
by Charlotte Danielson

Vol. 3: High School Mathematics
by Charlotte Danielson and Elizabeth Marquez

Block Scheduling: A Catalyst for Change in High Schools
by Robert Lynn Canady and Michael D. Rettig

Teaching in the Block
edited by Robert Lynn Canady and Michael D. Rettig

Educational Technology: Best Practices from America's Schools
by William C. Bozeman and Donna J. Baumbach

The Educator's Brief Guide to Computers in the Schools
by Eugene F. Provenzo, Jr.

Handbook of Educational Terms and Applications
by Arthur K. Ellis and Jeffrey T. Fouts

Research on Educational Innovations, 2d ed.
by Arthur K. Ellis and Jeffrey T. Fouts

Research on School Restructuring
by Arthur K. Ellis and Jeffrey T. Fouts

Hands-on Leadership Tools for Principals
by Ray Calabrese, Gary Short, and Sally Zepeda

The Principal as Steward
by Jack McCall

The Principal's Edge
by Jack McCall

Leadership: A Relevant and Practical Role for Principals
by Gary M. Crow, L. Joseph Matthews, and Lloyd E. McCleary

Directory of Innovations in Elementary Schools
by Jane McCarthy and Suzanne Still

**The School Portfolio:
A Comprehensive Framework for School Improvement**
by Victoria L. Bernhardt

The Administrator's Guide to School-Community Relations
by George E. Pawlas

Innovations in Parent and Family Involvement
by William Rioux and Nancy Berla

**The Performance Assessment Handbook
Bringing the NCTM Standards to Life**
by Lisa B. Owen and Charles E. Lamb

Mathematics the Write Way
by Marilyn S. Neil

School-to-Work
by Arnold H. Packer and Marion W. Pines

The Educator's Guide to Implementing Outcomes
by William J. Smith

Schools for All Learners: Beyond the Bell Curve
by Renfro C. Manning

ABOUT THE AUTHORS

Don Bragaw is Professor Emeritus at East Carolina University. Formerly an elementary and secondary school social studies teacher, he has served on several other university faculties including Syracuse University; State University of New York at Binghamton; and West Florida University. Author of numerous articles on social studies education, he formerly served as the president of the National Council for the Social Studies and the Social Science Education Consortium. He has also served as a consultant to numerous school districts, foundations, and corporations.

Karen Dawkins is assistant director of the Science and Mathematics Education Center at East Carolina University. With more than 20 years of science-teaching experience at the high school level, she now designs and implements professional development programs for K-12 science and mathematics teachers. She has directed 25 funded projects during the past 5 years.

Allan A. Glatthorn is Distinguished Research Professor of Education at East Carolina University where he teaches graduate courses in curriculum and instruction. He was a high school teacher, principal, and supervisor, and also served on the faculty of the Graduate School of Education of the University of Pennsylvania. Author of more than 20 professional books, he has served as a curriculum consultant to more than 100 school systems.

John Parker is assistant superintendent for curriculum and instruction in Roanoke Rapids (NC) Graded School District. He was a high school mathematics teacher in Virginia and North Carolina for 18 years before working in a variety of curriculum support positions at the district level. He currently serves as president of the Eastern Region of the North Carolina Council of Teachers of Mathematics. He was recently president of the North Carolina Council of Supervisors of Mathematics.

ACKNOWLEDGMENTS

We express our great indebtedness to the teachers in the Roanoke-Rapids School District who gave unselfishly of their time to try out these ideas. Under John Parker's leadership, they did an excellent job of using these ideas to develop their own approach and produce their own materials. We also wish to express our indebtedness to Robert Sickles, our publisher at Eye On Education, who strongly encouraged us to pursue the development of these ideas and share them with the profession. Finally, the work has profited from the helpful comments of Jay McTighe and Lucille Daniel.

TABLE OF CONTENTS

1

UNDERSTANDING THE ACHIEVEMENT CYCLE

This book explains a systematic approach to curriculum, assessment, instruction, and learning called the *achievement cycle*. This first chapter defines that term and its related concepts, provides the background knowledge for using the achievement cycle in the school system or classroom, and presents an overview of the rest of the book.

CLARIFYING THE ESSENTIAL CONCEPTS

It is essential to understand the key concepts used throughout the book, because several terms are often used in a confusing manner.

THE ACHIEVEMENT CYCLE

The achievement cycle, the key concept that undergirds this work, is defined here as the close interactive relationships of four key elements: standards-based curricula; performance evaluation; assessment-driven instruction (ADI); and authentic learning. Figure 1.1, on the next page, shows the cycle in diagrammatic form.

As Figure 1.1 suggests, the central aim of all curricula, assessments, and instruction (the contributing components) is authentic learning (the central outcome). In general, the cycle begins with curriculum, proceeds to performance assessments based on that curriculum, and then moves to assessment-driven instruction, as the optimal means of accomplishing authentic learning. However, the diagram is also intended to suggest that the three contributing elements can be ordered in several sequences, in a recursive manner.

FIGURE 1.1. THE ACHIEVEMENT CYCLE

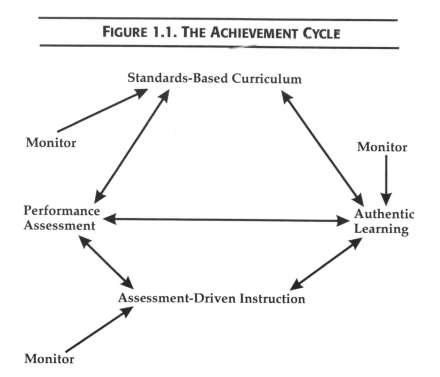

Thus, one might begin with assessments, derive the curricula from them, and then move to assessment-driven instruction. The essential element is the congruence of the three contributing components and a focus on the learning outcome.

Note also that Figure 1.1 emphasizes the importance of ongoing monitoring of both the contributing elements and the central outcome. As Palmer (1996) points out, such continuous monitoring is essential if the achievement cycle is to be effective in producing authentic learning. Such monitoring can occur through the teacher's observation of students, the analysis of student performance results, a critique of curriculum documents, an assessment of the teacher's plans, and the principal's observations of teacher performance. This continuous monitoring through these processes addresses such questions as:

- ♦ Does the curriculum reflect and embody the best current standards?

♦ Do the performance assessments constitute valid measures of student mastery of the curriculum?

♦ Are teachers devoting sufficient time to teaching to the performance tasks?

♦ Do performance results indicate that authentic learning is taking place?

STANDARDS-BASED CURRICULA

Standards-based curricula are curricula based on content standards as explicated by experts in the field. As Kendall and Marzano (1996) explain, content standards identify what students should know and be able to do; performance standards explicate the level of achievement expected for each content standard. The recommendation here is that school systems should develop their own content standards by drawing from and building on the standards developed by the several professional associations and state education agencies. (See Chapter 2 for a full explanation of the process.)

PERFORMANCE ASSESSMENTS AND RELATED TERMS

Such terms as *authentic assessment, performance evaluation,* and *portfolio assessment* are widely used at this time—and are often used in confusing ways. It therefore makes sense to clarify some key distinctions, as the terms are used in this work.

The basic concept is *assessment of student learning.* This is the broad term to denote the process of gathering data from multiple sources to make a judgment about student learning. The assessment process can take many forms such as:

♦ observation

♦ interview

♦ discussion

♦ examination of student work and products

♦ test of knowledge

♦ inspection of student performances and demonstrations

(See Linn & Baker, 1996; Chittenden, 1991.)

Performance assessment is one type of assessment of student learning. This book uses a definition suggested by Meyer (1992): a performance assessment is one that involves situations in which students must construct responses that illustrate their ability to apply knowledge. As Gooding (1994) notes, a performance assessment should have these characteristics.

- Longitudinal: Assesses student learning over an extended period of time.
- Authentic: Includes knowledge and skills needed for success outside of school.
- Open: Is based on standards and criteria known in advance by students, teachers, and parents.
- Is nonbiased: Allows use of processes that do not discriminate unfairly with respect to students' learning styles, backgrounds, and cultures.
- Requires the use of generative knowledge: Requires students to produce knowledge and use it in solving problems.
- Is process-oriented: Requires students to produce a product or performance.
- Is student-oriented: Involves students in self-assessment and in the development of assessment measures.

Authentic assessment is often used synonymously with *performance assessment*. However, Meyer makes a useful distinction, limiting *authentic assessment* to assessment processes that involve a real-life situation. Thus, a performance assessment might ask students to write a speech that could be delivered to the town council; an authentic assessment would require them to present the speech to the council.

Performance task is a complex open-ended problem posed for the student to solve as a means of demonstrating mastery; the performance tasks constitute the bases for the performance assessment. Marzano and Kendall (1996) identify these defining characteristics of a performance task:

- requires knowledge to be applied to a specific situation
- provides necessary guidance and information to complete the task
- specifies learning context (independent, pairs, small groups)
- specifies how students will demonstrate their findings or solution

This endorsement of performance assessments is not to suggest that they are without their own problems. Researchers have noted several limitations of performance assessments in general, especially when used for high stakes accountability. Mehrens (1991) points out that they have difficulty meeting the five criteria of administrative feasibility, professional credibility, public acceptability, legal defensibility, and economic affordability. Gearhart and Herman (1995) note that one difficulty in assessing student portfolios is that the portfolios reflect not only a student's competence but also the amount and quality of support from others such as teachers and peers. And Guskey (1996) reports on one doctoral study that concluded that the use of performance assessments resulted in only minor changes in the way teachers taught. Teachers interviewed reported that they did not have sufficient training to change their basic pedagogical strategies.

ASSESSMENT-DRIVEN INSTRUCTION

Assessment-driven instruction (ADI) is teaching and planning for teaching that are based on, derived from, and focused on performance assessment. ADI coaches students to prepare them for the performance task. To understand the uniqueness of ADI, consider the three contributing elements of classroom life: curriculum, instruction, and assessment. Both ADI and the conventional model begin with the curriculum as teachers decide what to teach. In the conventional model, teachers next instruct students and then develop and implement assessment measures. In the ADI model, the performance assessment is designed and then teachers instruct accordingly, coaching students to perform well on that measure.

One focus of this book, therefore, is on how teachers can use ADI to improve student performance on performance assessments.

TEACHING TO THE TEST AND ADI

Many teachers "teach to the test," preparing students to take such high-stakes examinations as standardized tests, state accountability tests, district-developed graduation tests, and teacher-made tests. (See, for example, Herman & Golan, 1991.) While ADI may seem like teaching to the test, there are some key differences. To understand those differences consider these two classroom illustrations.

TEACHING TO THE TEST

Students will have to take a short-answer objective test assessing their knowledge of the legislative process as employed in their state. A typical question asks students to define *bill* and *law*. The specific content of the test is confidential, with the test administered under conditions of high security. The teacher has identified the questions the test is likely to ask by reviewing previous editions of the test. The teacher prepares practice material on test-like items. Students spend most of their class time completing the practice exercises and checking their answers.

ASSESSMENT-DRIVEN INSTRUCTION

The teacher has developed a performance assessment: groups of students will develop an action plan to persuade the state legislature to enact legislation for solving a community problem the students have identified. The students' action plans will be presented to the state legislator representing that district who has agreed to judge the plans on the basis of their likely effectiveness. The teacher has explained the performance assessment to the students and has provided them with the criteria the legislator will use in assessing the action plans. The class is organized into four groups, each of which will identify a problem and develop its own action plan. The teacher helps the groups use class time to analyze the problem, understand the legislative process as it really works, and develop a feasible and realistic plan.

THE FUNDAMENTAL DIFFERENCE

Notice that the fundamental difference involves the nature of the assessment. If the assessment is concerned only with knowledge, the teacher figures out which terms will be tested, uses direct instruction and drill-and-practice to teach the terms, helps students memorize definitions, and checks their learning with practice tests. Such teaching to the test when accompanied by an emphasis on teacher accountability has several negative consequences. The curriculum is narrowed to what is likely to appear on the test; learning is fragmented, with students concentrating on bits and pieces of knowledge isolated from a real context; teaching is didactic; and the learning process bores the students. (For a detailed picture of such classrooms see McNeil 1986.) Many would consider such test preparation as professionally unethical. (See, for example, Mehrens & Kaminski, 1989.)

On the other hand, if an authentic performance assessment has been developed more exciting teaching and learning are likely to occur. In the example given, if the teacher and the students know that a feasible and effective action plan is to be presented, then the teacher plans for learning activities that will help students make the necessary preparations—identifying the problem, searching the knowledge base, interviewing legislators, developing a schedule, and evaluating the details of the plan.

Several studies conclude that performance assessments have many positive effects: students acquire in-depth knowledge; students demonstrate more interest in and more positive attitudes toward learning; students use higher thought processes. (See Gooding, 1994; Newmann, Secada, & Wehlage, 1995; Kattri, Kane, & Reeve, 1995.) Also, preparing students for performance assessments is clearly ethical, because the nature of the performance assessment is a matter of public knowledge, and the evaluators assume that the students have been adequately prepared.

RATIONALE FOR USING ADI

As explained more fully in later chapters, ADI should be structured so that it only requires about 60% of the available classroom time. Because it will occupy much of the available time, educators should be able to present a convincing rationale to teachers, parents, and students. If the performance assessment is a valid measure of the mastery of complex skills and knowledge, and if ADI has been implemented effectively, then these assumptions are plausible.

- ◆ ADI will enable students to perform better on real-life learning tasks. While no one can ever guarantee learner outcomes, the research generally indicates that effective instruction achieves its intended outcomes. (See, for example, Walberg, 1995.) Thus, there is greater likelihood of transfer of learning, because the assessment is based on a real-life context.

- ◆ ADI will result in quality teaching. Rather than fostering the continued use of drill books and practice exercises, ADI helps teachers plan for learning that involves students in meaningful and purposeful problem-solving activities. Effectively applied, ADI meets the three criteria for what Newmann, Marks, and Gamoran (1995) call "authentic pedagogy": it requires students to produce knowledge, applying it in creating products; it emphasizes disciplined inquiry; and it has value beyond school.

- ◆ ADI will result in more effective schools. If applied effectively across the school, ADI will strengthen and bring into congruence several of the key elements of effective schools: a coordinated curriculum; effective teaching; and authentic assessment. (See Cotton, 1995.)

Delineating these advantages is not to suggest that ADI is without its challenges. It requires greater skill on the part of teachers. Developing valid performance assessments is a complex skill, one that teachers can acquire only with a great deal of assistance and support. It asks the principal to develop a new approach to staff development and teacher supervision, one that provides the needed coaching and feedback. And it requires students to perform in new and challenging ways. They have to think critically, solve complex problems, and communicate their results.

AUTHENTIC LEARNING

As noted earlier, the central purpose of curricula, assessments, and instruction is improving authentic learning. The characteristics of authentic learning are presented in Figure 1.2, on the next page, in contrast with the elements of what is called here "standard school learning." (The key elements of authentic learning are explained more fully in Chapter 5; the elements have been derived from the literature, chiefly Brooks & Brooks, 1993; Marzano, Pickering, & McTighe, 1993; and Newmann, Secada, & Wehlage, 1995.) As Figure 1.2 suggests, authentic learning is higher-order learning used in solving contextualized problems; it is more challenging and complex than standard school learning.

ORGANIZING FOR THE TASKS

How do you accomplish all the critical tasks involved in planning for and implementing the achievement cycle? Because districts vary considerably in size and resources, no single model of organizational structures will work for all systems. All that matters is that the school system effectively and efficiently accomplishes its goals of producing excellent standards-based curricula, high quality assessments, and developing teachers who foster authentic learning. (See Chapter 10 for a detailed discussion of implementation strategies.)

Figure 1.3, on page 13, shows graphically one organizational structure that has worked well in several curriculum projects. (See Glatthorn, 1994.) Note that the organizational chart maintains the integrity of the traditional line of authority—from board, to superintendent, to principal, to teachers.

FIGURE 1.2. AUTHENTIC LEARNING AND STANDARD SCHOOL LEARNING COMPARED

ASPECT	STANDARD SCHOOL LEARNING	AUTHENTIC LEARNING
Learning Purpose	Pass examinations	Deepen understanding, solve problems
Approach to Knowledge	Reproduce knowledge to demonstrate learning	Produce knowledge in order to solve problems
Substance of Learning	Facts, data, algorithms, formulas	Key concepts, strategies
Thought Processes Emphasized	Recall, comprehension	Analysis, synthesis, evaluation
Depth of Learning	Shallow, to achieve coverage	Deep, to achieve understanding
Type of Problems Presented	Contrived, not in context	Meaningful, contextualized
Type of Responses	Short answer	Elaborated, extended communication
Importance of Metacognition	Limited	Crucial
Type of Evaluation	True/false, multiple choice	Performance assessment
Concern for Affective and Cognitive	Focus on cognitive only	Aware of affective component of learning

FIGURE 1.3. ORGANIZATIONAL STRUCTURES

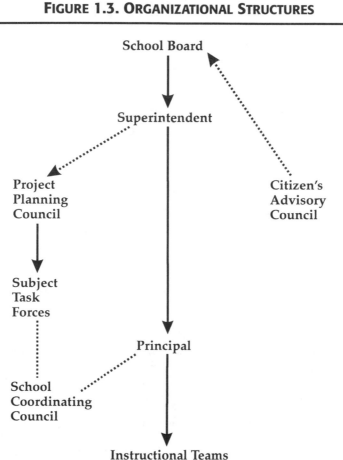

The *Project Planning Council* (PPC) is the professional steering group responsible for scheduling, planning, and monitoring all the projects associated with the achievement cycle reform. It should be a representative group, chaired by the assistant superintendent for curriculum and instruction, that includes representatives of these constituencies: central office staff, school administrators, and classroom teachers. It has several responsibilities including these:

- Communicating to the superintendent, maintaining a liaison with the Citizens Advisory Council, and communicating with the public about the project.

- Appointing all the subject task forces.

- Scheduling and coordinating all individual projects.

- Developing a project budget and providing resources needed by the task forces.

- Training the principals and central office supervisors for their new roles.

- Developing standards that cut across and supplement those for the separate subjects such as those for Life Skills. (See Kendall & Marzano, 1996.)

- Determining a standard format and content for the curriculum guide.

- Coordinating the school-based and subject-based staff development for all aspects of the project.

The *Citizen's Advisory Council* reports to the board so as not to dilute the board's ultimate authority. It should include representatives from the community who reflect the community's diversity and have strong relationships with it. Their function is to provide input to the board about community concerns relative to the project, to provide a forum for community members to raise concerns, and to review all documents produced by the project. It is recommended that the citizen's council should act in an advisory manner only. While some districts prefer to give this group decision-making power, doing so may undercut the board's legitimate authority. The assistant superintendent for curriculum and instruction should be an ex officio member who provides liaison between the curriculum council and the advisory council. Many district leaders reject the recommendation that such groups should be established, believing that citizen representation should be the sole responsibility of the school board.

The *Subject Task Forces* do the specific work involved with each of the subjects. Task force membership should include supervisors, school administrators, and classroom teachers with in-depth knowledge of the subject. All their work involves the full scope of one subject of the district's educational program, from Kindergarten to Grade 12. Their responsibilities include:

- Identifying the standards the district will use in its curriculum work.

- Identifying the school-level or grade-level benchmarks that make up the standards. (More detail about these matters is provided in Chapter 3.)

- Develop the district's performance assessments for that subject.

- Provide the necessary training for the instructional teams.

Larger districts with greater personnel resources may wish to appoint three K-12 councils to provide leadership in the three components of the achievement cycle: curriculum council; assessment council; and instruction council. These councils would report to the Project Planning Council. In addition to these districtwide groups, each school would have its own coordinating council (whose functions may be discharged by any existing schoolwide committee) and the instructional teams (organized by grade-level at the elementary and middle levels and by department at the high school).

Each district should develop its own organizational structures. All that matters is that these complex tasks be carried out efficiently and effectively. Smaller districts that want a simpler structure might consider organizing interested teachers into study groups, providing them with the needed training, and letting the project grow of its own accord.

OVERVIEW OF THE BOOK

Chapter 3 explains how to use curriculum standards in developing the curriculum. It also explains a process for designing performance assessments based on that curriculum. Chapter 4 explains one process for planning and delivering assessment-driven instruction. Chapter 5 discusses authentic learning. Chapters 6 through 9 explain the application of the achievement cycle to the four academic subjects that make up the heart of the school's educational program. The last chapter, Chapter 10, explains the support system needed to make the model effective.

REFERENCES

Brooks, J.G. & Brooks, M.G. (1993). *In search of understanding: The case for constructivist classrooms.* Alexandria, VA: Association for Supervision and Curriculum Development.

Chittenden, E. (1991). Authentic assessment, evaluation, and documentation of student performance. In V. Perrone (Ed.), *Expanding student assessment* (pp. 22–31). Alexandria, VA: Association for Supervision and Curriculum Development.

Cotton, K. (1995). *Effective schooling practices: A research synthesis, 1995 update.* Portland, OR: Northwest Regional Educational Laboratory.

Gearhart, M. & Herman, J.L. (1995). Portfolio assessment: Whose work is it? *Evaluation Comment.* Los Angeles: Center for the Study of Evaluation.

Glatthorn, A.A. (1994). *Developing the quality curriculum.* Alexandria, VA: Association for Supervision and Curriculum Development.

Gooding, K. (1994, April). *Teaching to the test: The influence of alternative modes of assessment on teachers' instructional strategies.* Paper presented at annual meeting of the American Educational Research Association, New Orleans.

Guskey, T.R. (1996). What you assess may not be what you get. In R.E. Blum & J.A. Arter (Eds.), *Student performance in an era of restructuring* (pp. IV-8-1–4). Alexandria, VA: Association for Supervision and Curriculum Development.

Herman, J. & Golan, S. (1991). *Effects of standardized tests on teaching and learning* (CSE Technical Report #334). Los Angeles, CA: National Center for Research on Evaluation, Standards, and Student Testing.

Kattri, N., Kane, M.B., & Reeve, A.L. (1995). How perform-ance assessments affect teaching and learning. *Educational Leadership, 53* (3), 80–83.

Kendall, J.S., & Marzano, R.J. (1996). *Content knowledge.* Aurora, CO: Mid-Continent Regional Educational Laboratory.

Linn, R.L. & Baker, E.L. (1996). Can performance-based stu-dent assessments be psychometrically sound? In J.B. Baron & D.P. Wolf (Eds.), *Performance-based student assess-ment: Challenges and responsibilities* (pp. 84–103). Chicago: University of Chicago Press.

Marzano, R.J. & Kendall, J.S. (1996). *A comprehensive guide to designing standards-based districts, schools, and classrooms.* Alexandria, VA: Association for Supervision and Curricu-lum Development.

Marzano, R.J., Pickering, D., & McTighe, J. (1993). *Assessing student outcomes.* Alexandria, VA: Association for Super-vision and Curriculum Development.

McNeil, L.M. (1986). *Contradictions of control: School structure and school knowledge.* New York: Routledge & Kegan Paul.

Mehrens, W.A. (1991, April). *Using performance assessment for accountability purposes.* Paper presented at annual meeting of the American Educational Research Association, Chicago.

Mehrens, W.A., & Kaminski, J. (1989). Methods for improv-ing standardized test scores: Fruitful, fruitless, or fraudu-lent? *Educational Measurement: Issues and Practices, 8,* 14–22.

Meyer, C.A. (1992). What's the difference between authentic and performance assessment? *Educational Leadership, 49* (8), 39–40.

Newmann, F.M., Marks, H.M., & Gamoran, A. (1995). *Authen-tic pedagogy and student achievement.* Madison, WI: Center on Organization and Restructuring of Schools, University of Wisconsin-Madison.

Newmann, F.M., Secada, W.G, & Wehlage, G.G. (1995). *A guide to authentic instruction and assessment.* Madison, WI: Wisconsin Center for Educational Research, University of Wisconsin-Madison.

Palmer, J. (1996). Integrating assessment and instruction: Continuous monitoring. In R.E. Blum & J.A. Arter (Eds.), *Student performance assessment in an era of restructuring* (pp. IV-6-1–6). Alexandria, VA: Association for Supervision and Curriculum Development.

Walberg, H.J. (1995). Generic practices. In G. Cawelti (Ed.), *Handbook of research on improving student achievement* (pp. 7–20). Arlington, VA: Educational Research Service.

2

DEVELOPING A STANDARDS-BASED CURRICULUM

As explained in Chapter 1, the achievement cycle begins with curriculum and moves from there to assessment and then to instruction. While it is possible to design performance assessments without reference to the curriculum, doing so would probably result in a collection of isolated performances with no guarantee that they represent a comprehensive educational program. The discussion that follows explains one process for developing a standards-based curriculum. Although this process has worked well in practice, there are others that could be used. Chapter 10 includes several specific recommendations for implementing these steps.

UNDERSTAND KEY CONCEPTS

There are many ways to develop the curriculum as the basis for assessments. At this juncture the best basis available is the use of *content standards*. A growing body of expert opinion supports standards-based reform as the best way to improve student achievement. (See, for example, Cohen, 1995; McLaughlin & Shepard, 1995; and Marzano & Kendall, 1996.) To know how to use content standards, you need to discriminate among several related terms. As Cohen (1995) notes, the field of standards is so new that terms are often used in a confusing and muddled manner. The following definitions are used throughout this book.

CONTENT STANDARDS

Content standards (sometimes termed *curriculum standards*) are statements of the skills and knowledge that students should know in a given subject by the end of their secondary schooling. This definition attempts to resolve three issues often debated in the field. First, it focuses on what the learner is to do. Some documents define standards in terms of what the curriculum should include. For example, the social studies standards developed by the National Council for the Social Studies (1994) emphasize the curriculum—and then state the learner outcomes. Here is one example from the NCSS report:

> Social studies programs should include experiences that provide for the study of *how people create and change structures of power, authority, and governance*, so that the learner can.... (Italics in original; p. 39)

Second, the definition specifies standards based on a single school subject. Some critics express concern that limiting standards to a given subject area inhibits the development of interdisciplinary units. However, Marzano and Kendall (1996) are convincing when they argue that those interested in integration will get better results if they begin with the separate subject standards and then integrate where appropriate. Finally, the definition posits a K-12 spectrum. Marzano and Kendall note that it may be desirable to separate high school standards from those for K-8. However, setting standards for grades K-12 would seem to result in a better coordinated and more seamless program.

Content benchmarks (often referred to as "benchmarks") are components of the content standards identified for a particular grade level (such as Grade 6) or level of schooling (such as Grades 6–8). Here, for example, is one of the middle grades benchmarks from the NCSS social studies report.

> a. Examine persistent issues involving the rights, roles, and status of the individual in relation to the general welfare. (p. 39)

PERFORMANCE STANDARDS

Performance standards are the "indices of quality that specify how adept or competent a student must be" (National

Education Goals Panel, 1993, p. iii). Here, for example, is the performance standard that might be used to assess students' performance with the benchmark noted above.

> Examines issue of right to free speech, explaining importance of that right in a democracy and noting limitations established by the courts.

OPPORTUNITY TO LEARN STANDARDS

Opportunity to learn standards are specifications of the resources needed by all students to achieve the content standards. As noted by McLaughlin and Shepard (1995), they include well-prepared teachers, appropriate instructional materials, a safe school environment, and effective instructional activities. Ignoring the opportunity standards while emphasizing content standards can result in inequitable systems.

DEVELOP THE CONTENT STANDARDS

The first major component of the development process is to identify the content standards.

DEVELOP A COMPREHENSIVE SET OF CONTENT STANDARDS

The first step in the process is to develop a comprehensive set of standards for a given subject. (The discussion that follows assumes that each of the Subject Task Forces will be accomplishing the tasks listed and that the reader is a task force member.) Begin by listing the standards developed by your state department of education. Every state except Wyoming has produced or plans to produce content standards for each subject area. (See Gandal, 1996.) Gandal notes that these state standards are of very uneven quality. For example, he reports this evaluation with respect to the materials produced by the North Carolina Department of Public Instruction: "Though the math document is particularly strong, the rest of the subjects are not strong enough..." (p. 27).

After examining the state standards, you should also give special attention to any state tests that must be administered in your schools. The state tests are an important source for determining the standards that really matter, especially if the results will be used to evaluate schools or teachers.

Next, check the standards produced by the appropriate professional organization. Every professional organization concerned with school subjects has produced its own recommended standards for that particular field. Here, again, you will find an unevenness of quality. For example, the standards developed by the National Council of Teachers of English and the International Reading Association (1996) have been widely criticized for being too general and devoid of content. (For a discussion of this issue, see Maloney, 1997; Stotsky, 1997.) You also need to be aware of the ideological controversy surrounding some of these standards. For example, Ravitch (1994) has criticized the history standards for minimizing commonalities that hold the nation together, giving too much emphasis to the differences that divide. To simplify the review of professional standards, you may wish to consult the Kendall and Marzano (1996) compilation; it is an excellent collection of the professional standards developed by that date.

Next, you should examine your district's curriculum guide. If it is reasonably current and has been getting good results, you can readily derive the standards by generalizing from the specific objectives that are usually included in such works. Here, for example, is an excerpt from an English language arts guide produced by a local school system.

> Define literary terms: *metaphor, imagery, simile, irony.*

Here is the standard that might be derived from this and other related objectives.

> Interpret imaginative works in a variety of media, using such appropriate literary concepts as *metaphor, imagery, simile, irony.*

Observe that the standard is much more general than the objective.

If teachers are satisfied with the quality of the textbooks and other resources, you should consult those textbooks and resources. While textbooks do not provide a sound basis for curriculum, excellent texts and other resources contribute to the opportunity to learn. For example, a widely used biology text includes several chapters on chordates, suggesting that the study of this phylum should be included in the standards for this subject.

Finally, check your district's tests. If they are current, are of high quality, and are likely to be used in the near future, they can give you some leads about standards you might have missed.

At this stage your concern is to develop a comprehensive list, one that includes standards from several sources. One useful way of assembling such a list is to develop a large chart similar to the one shown in Figure 2.1 on the next page. Note that it groups the standards by *strands*. The strands are the divisions of the subject as the subject is usually conceptualized by experts in the field. You might have one standard for one strand and several for another. Note also that each subject has its own strand structure. The problem is an especially complex one in social studies because this broad subject includes separate subjects such as civics, economics, and political science.

In Figure 2.1, each of the sources is listed across the top. The "Teacher Priority" column is explained later in this chapter.

REFINE THE COMPREHENSIVE LIST

Once the comprehensive list has been developed, the next step is to refine it. You refine it by first eliminating any duplications of standards that might have been inadvertently included. In developing that refined list, you should also eliminate any standards that seem too vague or have no relevance for your district. Here, for example, is a standard from the set produced by the National Council of Teachers of English and the International Reading Association (1996).

> Students participate as knowledgeable, reflective, creative, and critical members of a variety of literacy communities. (p. 25)

This standard may be too vague for your project.

FIGURE 2.1. CHART FOR COMPREHENSIVE LIST OF STANDARDS

SUBJECT: SCIENCE

Strands & standards	STATE STDS	STATE TESTS	PROF STDS	DIST GUID	TEXT	DIST TEST	TCHR PRIOR
Earth and Space							
1. Understands features of Earth.	X	X	X	X		X	1.5
2.							

CODE: STATE STDS, appears in state standards; STATE TESTS, tested in state tests; PROF STDS, recommended by professional groups; DIST GUID, included in district curriculum guide; TEXT, included in adopted texts; DIST TEST, tested in district testing program; TCHR PRIOR, the priority assigned by teachers.

Next you should combine any that seem very similar. For example, here are two standards from the music standards developed by the Consortium of National Arts Education Associations (1994).

Understanding relationships between music, the other arts, and disciplines outside the arts.

Understanding music in relation to history and culture. (p. 63)

Those two might be combined into one standard, as follows:

Understanding the relationships between music, other disciplines, history, and culture.

SECURE TEACHER INPUT

The next step is to ask teachers to prioritize the refined list as they reflect about their experience, their knowledge of the subject, and their understanding of their students. How you get teacher input depends on the size of the district. If the district is a small one, you can survey all teachers who teach that subject. If the district is a large one, you might consider having teachers in each building discuss the standards, with a representative reporting results to the task force. In either case, the teachers should receive preliminary and systematic training with respect to the task, so that their input is more meaningful. Also, the survey should be completed at a school-based faculty meeting so that teachers take the task seriously.

A survey form can be designed from the refined list, with directions similar to these:

The Mathematics Task Force would like your input about the standards we should use in our work in curriculum and assessment. Below are listed all the standards we have compiled from several sources. Now we would like your judgment about the importance of each. Reflect about your experience, your knowledge of the subject, and your understanding of your students. In the space provided next to each standard, circle one of these numbers to indicate the priority you would assign:

1: Top priority. This standard is really important for all my students.

2: Middle priority. This standard is of moderate importance for all my students.

3: Low priority: This standard is of low importance for all my students.

The task force can then calculate the mean score for the teachers' prioritizing, noting the result on the chart.

DEVELOP THE FINAL DRAFT OF THE STANDARDS

The task force can then review all the data recorded on the chart to determine which standards will govern curriculum development and assessment in that subject. They should also reflect about their own knowledge and experience. In doing so, they should keep in mind the importance of depth of coverage, in contrast to wide coverage. F. James Rutherford, director of the widely respected "Project 2061" in science, reports that his group found that high school textbooks list 120 different technical terms about the cell, but that the group determined that 11 words were sufficient (as reported in U.S. Department of Education, 1995.) Rutherford added this comment: "If you concentrate on what goes on in the cell...you come out with a deeper understanding" (p. 11).

In finalizing this review, the task force should divide the list of standards into two groups: Essential Standards and Enrichment Standards. The Essential Standards are those that all students are expected to master. The Enrichment Standards are those that the teacher may include if there is time. In general, the final list of standards should include approximately 8 to 12 Essential Standards for each subject and 6 to 10 Enrichment Standards. The Kendall/Marzano collection has a range of 4 to 29 essential standards, although they recommend 10.

Obviously, the number of standards to list as "Essential" is an important issue that requires careful study by the task force. Because standards-driven curricula are a relatively recent phenomenon, there is no research yet to support the foregoing recommendations. The recommendations result instead from a review of best practice, a careful analysis of the time available, and an awareness of the need for depth.

IDENTIFY THE BENCHMARKS

The final list of standards becomes the basis for identifying the benchmarks.

As explained earlier, these are the specific outcomes for a given standard for a specific grade level. Some professional standards, such as those produced by NCTE/IRA, are not accompanied by benchmarks. The rationale is that these matters should be resolved at the classroom level by teachers sensitive to students' special needs. The Kendall/Marzano compilation specifies for each standard four levels of benchmarks: Level I, Grades K-2; Level II, Grades 3–5; Level III, Grades 6–8; Level IV, Grades 9–12.

The issue of whether to specify benchmarks by grade level or by schooling level should be decided by the Project Planning Council. We recommend that benchmarks for each grade level be specified so as to provide clearer guidance to teachers and eliminate unnecessary repetition.

REVIEW DECISIONS ABOUT CONTENT EMPHASIS

The next task is to determine the content emphasis for each grade level. To begin the process, the task force should review the content emphases for each grade in the existing educational program. For example, in the social studies curriculum, most school districts emphasize U.S. history in Grades 5, 8, and 11. In mathematics, pre-Algebra is often taught in Grade 8. In science, Biology is usually emphasized in Grade 10. These content decisions obviously influence the grade placement of benchmarks, as explained in the next section.

Where content is repeated in two or more grade levels, the task force may decide to provide developmental variation in a subject such as social studies, to avoid undue repetition. Here, for example, is one division that seems to work well.

Grade 5 social studies: U.S. history from the early explorations to 1861.

Grade 8 social studies: U.S. history from the Civil War to the Great Depression.

Grade 11 social studies: U.S. history from World War II to the present.

IDENTIFY STANDARDS FOR CONTINUING DEVELOPMENT

The next step is to review the list of Essential Standards to identify any that should be emphasized and reinforced at several grade levels rather than being benchmarked for a specific grade level; such standards are termed *standards for continuing development*. Many of the standards produced by both state departments of education and professional organizations identify affective outcomes, attitudes, behaviors, and experiences that should not be confined to one grade level but that should be nurtured on every appropriate occasion. For example, many state standards include a writing standard that is phrased in this manner:

Use the writing process to communicate effectively.

Obviously, this standard should be given attention in every grade, many times each year—not taught once and then forgotten.

Another example comes from the art standards. The standards developed by the Consortium of National Arts Education Associations (1994) uses an arrow to indicate that a standard or benchmark is "...not repeated, but students at this grade level are expected to achieve that standard, demonstrating higher levels of skill..." (p. 87).

While this practice of noting standards for continuing development seems useful, developers should be certain that the practice does not result in excessive repetition from grade to grade. In general, the task force should attempt to develop a developmental set of benchmarks that reflects increasing complexity and maturity.

These standards for continuing development should be listed separately in the publications noted later, with a prefatory comment to this effect:

The following Standards for Continuing Development should be given appropriate emphasis at each grade level. They are essential for all students but are not benchmarked because they need continuing development in all grades.

DECIDE HOW BENCHMARKS WILL BE IDENTIFIED

Two different approaches usable to identify benchmarks are (1) to have the task force make preliminary decisions and then solicit teacher review, and (2) to train the teachers and then ask them to identify the benchmarks, with the task force responsible for reviewing and refining teacher recommendations. Either approach works; the matter is best resolved at the local level, based on the resources available and staff competence. The following discussion assumes that the task force does the job initially.

ANALYZE THE CONSTRAINTS

The task force should turn its attention to the remaining Essential Standards, first examining the factors that constrain benchmark placement. The first constraint is the need for depth. The task force should continue to emphasize the importance of depth, even if it means sacrificing some coverage. Kendall and Marzano recommend an average of three benchmarks per grade for each standard. There would, of course, be some variation from this average, depending upon the age of the students and the complexity of the standard.

Second, the task force should consider time allocations as a constraint, remembering that the standards and their associated benchmarks should not occupy all the time allocated to that curricular area. Gandal (1995) recommends that the standards-based curriculum require only 60–80% of the available time. These matters are more fully discussed in the following chapters. The final constraint, as noted previously, is the content emphases for each grade and their influence on benchmark decisions.

DEVELOP INITIAL DRAFT

With these considerations in mind, the task force should review all the available sources that will influence the benchmarking task. These sources should prove useful: professional recommendations; state specifications; the existing district curriculum guide; the adopted textbooks; and state and district tests. If these sources do not provide sufficient guidance, the task force should do its own concept and task analysis, in essence answering a question of this type: "What should our 5th graders know in order to achieve this standard?"

In developing this initial draft of benchmarks, Kendall and Marzano recommend that local developers distinguish between *declarative knowledge* (termed *knowledge* in common parlance) and *procedural knowledge* (termed *skills* in everyday use). Declarative knowledge, as they use the term, includes terms, concepts, facts, episodes, generalizations, principles, time sequences, cause and effect sequences, principles, and generalizations; it is "knowing that...." Procedural knowledge includes algorithms, processes, strategies, heuristics, and techniques; it is "knowing how...." Your task force might decide to use simpler terms: *knowledge*, for *declarative knowledge*; and *skills*, for *procedural knowledge*. Or it might decide that the distinction is not important enough to add to an already complex process.

The task force should also keep in mind the significance of content placement. For example, Kendall and Marzano specify two social studies benchmarks for Grades 5 and 6, which relate to early European exploration. If your district's social studies curriculum places the early European discoverers in the curriculum for Grade 5, then both benchmarks should be assigned to Grade 5.

When the benchmarks have been tentatively allocated by the task force, it should then undertake its own evaluation before submitting the benchmarks to teachers for review. In undertaking this evaluation, the task force can use the criteria listed in Figure 2.2.

SECURE TEACHER REVIEW

The benchmarks developed by the task force should also be reviewed by classroom teachers for the grade level for which those teachers are responsible. All teachers who teach science in Grade 6, for example, should review the benchmarks for Grade 6 science to ensure that they are developmentally appropriate—challenging, but attainable with effort. The task force should review all teacher recommendations, determining which ones to include in the final revision.

FIGURE 2.2. CRITERIA FOR EVALUATING BENCHMARKS

Are the Benchmarks:

1. Few in number, so that mastery can be accomplished?
2. Developmentally appropriate—challenging but attainable with effort?
3. Specified clearly?
4. Progressive from grade to grade, building upon what has been learned before, without undue repetition?
5. Directly related to the standards?
6. Effectively distributed over the grades, so that one grade is not overloaded or underloaded?
7. Current, reflecting the recommendations of experts in the field, including experienced and knowledgeable teachers?
8. Congruent with content emphasis for that grade level?

DEVELOP THE FINAL PRODUCTS

When in final form, all these decisions should be placed on a large scope-and-sequence chart. Down the left side list the standards organized by strands. Indicate the grades across the top. In each resulting cell note the benchmarks for that grade and that standard. The advantage of the chart is that it shows at a glance how benchmarks develop from grade to grade.

That scope-and-sequence chart can then be used in developing a revised curriculum guide. Some districts prefer a "teacher-friendly" guide that includes only these components.

- A prefatory list of Standards for Continuing Development, those that will not be benchmarked.
- The Essential Standards.
- The grade-level benchmarks for the Essential Standards.

Others believe that a more detailed guide should be developed that includes these addtional components:

- enrichment standards and benchmarks
- philosophy of curriculum
- vision of curriculum
- educational goals
- review of the research
- teaching suggestions
- resources available
- assessment processes
- sample units

One of the critical issues with respect to the curriculum guide is whether it should include detailed *learning objectives* or whether this should be left in teachers' hands. The term *learning objectives,* as used here, means specific learner outcomes that are derived from benchmarks and used to facilitate the classroom learning processes.

To understand the importance of this issue, consider this benchmark for high school science, from Project 2061 (1993):

Knows that earthquakes often occur along the boundaries between colliding plates.

That benchmark should be further separated into its component learning objectives:

- Define *earthquake.*

- ◆ Explain the causes of earthquakes.
- ◆ Explain *Richter Scale* as an earthquake measure.
- ◆ Explain how earthquake-prone areas can best prepare.
- ◆ Explain what residents should do when an earthquake occurs.

The Project Planning Council should resolve this issue of curriculum guide content for all subject areas. The general recommendation is to keep the guide as simple as possible, giving teachers the opportunity to develop the components they need. (For an explanation of the teacher's role, see Glatthorn, 1994.)

One crucial curriculum task remains—developing assessment-based units. That task should be accomplished by classroom teachers (see Chapter 4).

SUMMARY OF THE PROCESSES

Because the process is a complex one, a summary of the key steps is provided in Figure 2.3 on the next page. Keep in mind that the Planning Council should develop its own process, one that reflects its priorities and its resources.

FIGURE 2.3. DEVELOPING A STANDARDS-BASED CURRICULUM

♦ Develop standards

1. Develop a comprehensive set of content standards, using multiple sources.

2. Refine the comprehensive list by eliminating and combining.

3. Secure teacher input to identify teacher priorities.

4. Use data to develop final draft of standards, divided into Essential Standards and Enrichment Standards.

♦ Develop benchmarks

1. Review decisions about content emphases.

2. Identify Standards for Continuing Development—Essential Standards that will not be benchmarked.

3. Decide how benchmarks will be initially identified—by task force or by teachers.

4. Develop initial draft of benchmarks, evaluating with criteria provided.

5. Secure teacher review; revise benchmarks as needed.

♦ Develop final products

1. Use standards and benchmarks to produce scope and sequence chart.

2. Decide on curriculum guide content.

3. Analyze benchmarks into learning objectives.

REFERENCES

Cohen, D. (1995). What standards for national standards? *Phi Delta Kappan, 76,* 751–757.

Consortium of National Arts Education Associations. (1994). *National standards for arts education.* Reston, VA: Author.

Gandal, M. (1995). Not all standards are created equal. *Educational Leadership, 52* (6), 16–21.

Gandal, M. (1996). *Making standards matter, 1996.* Washington, DC: American Federation of Teachers.

Glatthorn, A.A. (1994). *Developing the quality curriculum.* Alexandria, VA: Association for Supervision and Curriculum Development.

Kendall, J.S., & Marzano, R.J. (1996). *Content knowledge: A compendium of standards and benchmarks for K-12 education.* Alexandria, VA: Association for Supervision and Curriculum Development.

Maloney, H.B. (1997). The little standards that couldn't. *English Journal, 86* (1), 86–90.

Marzano, R.J., & Kendall, J.S. (1996). *A comprehensive guide to designing standards-based districts, schools, and classrooms.* Alexandria, VA: Association for Supervision and Curriculum Development.

McLaughlin, M.W., & Shepard, L.A. (1995). *Improving education through standards-based reform.* Stanford, CA: National Academy of Education.

National Council for the Social Studies. (1994). *Curriculum standards for social studies.* Washington, DC: Author.

National Council of Teachers of English and International Reading Association. (1996). *Standards for the English language arts.* Urbana, IL: Author.

National Education Goals Panel. (1993). *Handbook for local goals reports.* Washington, DC: Author.

Project 2061, American Association for the Advancement of Science. (1993). *Benchmarks for science literacy.* New York: Oxford University Press.

Ravitch, D. (1994, Dec. 7). Standards in U.S. history: An assessment. *Education Week,* pp. 48, 50.

Stotsky, S. (1997). *State English standards.* Washington, DC: Fordham Foundation.

U.S. Department of Education. (1995). *Teachers and Goals 2000: Leading the journey toward high standards for all teachers.* Washington, DC: Author.

3

DEVELOPING PERFORMANCE TASKS AND PERFORMANCE ASSESSMENTS

Once the curriculum decisions have been made, the performance tasks can be developed and the performance assessments administered. As explained in Chapter 1, the performance tasks are the complex open-ended problems that constitute the basis for performance assessment. In the organizational model we recommend (see Figure 1.3 on p. 13), the subject task force develops the performance tasks required for district testing and classroom teachers develop the performance tasks to be used in the classroom. The needed training and technical assistance are provided to both groups. This chapter emphasizes classroom tasks and assessments.

Several testing and measurements experts strongly recommend that the district tasks and assessments be reviewed for validity and reliability. The Project Planning Council can discharge this function, if they have the time and competence; otherwise, the district can contract with external consultants for these services.

ALLOCATE TASK DEVELOPMENT TO SCHOOLS

The discussion that follows focuses on the development of performance tasks by classroom teachers who constitute the instructional teams. However, before teams begin development of specific tasks, district leaders may wish to develop a comprehensive plan that assigns the tasks to the schools in the district. Such a plan facilitates cooperation between teams at different schools and avoids duplication of effort. The comprehensive plan should show each course for which performance tasks will be developed and which teams will be responsible. Figure 3.1, on the next page, shows how this information can be displayed. After the teacher-developed tasks have been evaluated and revised, store them in a central database, to be shared with all teachers who can use them.

DECIDE ABOUT CURRICULUM INTEGRATION

It is at this stage that school-based teams should decide if the performance tasks will focus on one school subject or integrate two or more subjects. The decision about the nature of the performance task determines the kinds of units developed. Although there is currently much interest in curriculum integration, some concerns about too much integration have been raised. For that reason, we recommend that the school faculty, under the leadership of the principal, determine the nature and extent of integration before the development of performance tasks and units.

ARGUMENTS SUPPORTING INTEGRATION

Several arguments have been advanced supporting the practice of combining two or more separate subjects. First, the research generally supports this type of integration. Vars (1991) points out that more than 90 studies comparing integrated curricula with traditional ones have concluded that students learn more with integrated approaches.

Several theoretical arguments are also advanced. Supporters point out that problems in the real world cannot be compartmentalized into one discipline. Solving a problem of water quality requires knowledge of science, mathematics, economics, and political science. They also note that student concerns (such as choosing a career) transcend the disciplines. Finally, they argue that preliminary research on the brain suggests that students learn better when learning is holistic, not fragmented.

ARGUMENTS QUESTIONING THE USE OF INTEGRATION

All curriculum experts are not convinced that integration is totally desirable. Gardner and Boix-Mansilla (1994) are persuasive in arguing for the importance of disciplinary knowledge, noting that students' access to disciplinary knowledge

FIGURE 3.1. ALLOCATION OF PERFORMANCE TASKS

Subject: Science

CRS/SCHL	ADAMS ELEM	DAVIS ELEM	GROVE ELEM	ADEN MIDDL	TOWN MIDDL	EAST HIGH	WEST HIGH
GR 1	X						
GR 2		X					
GR 3			X				
GR 6				X			
GR 7					X		
BIOL						X	
CHEM							X

To conserve space, only selected courses are shown.

is essential in acquiring a quality education. Their position is supported by Roth's (1994) experience in working with teachers to develop an integrated unit. She concluded that the thematic unit on "1492" resulted in very superficial knowledge on the part of students. Other advocates of subject-focused curricula, such as Bruner (1960), note that each discipline has its own way of knowing, its own standards for validating knowledge and its own key concepts. Brophy and Alleman (1991) caution that many of the integrated units they have examined were poorly designed collections of activities, only loosely connected.

Given the current state of knowledge about curriculum integration, it seems wise for the principal to work with the faculty in deciding how and to what extent they will want to integrate their curriculum.

MAKE PRELIMINARY PLANS

Now each instructional team, with its assignments from the task force, takes over. Before developing the performance tasks required, each team needs to make some preliminary decisions.

DEVELOP A COMPREHENSIVE PLAN

The first planning responsibility of the instructional teams is to develop a comprehensive plan that shows them and their colleagues which performance tasks will be developed. Before developing individual performance tasks, they should have a systematic plan for the entire project.

In developing such a comprehensive plan, they should keep in mind several assumptions:

- ♦ Standards-driven curricula should occupy only part of the entire instructional program. Experience suggests that a range of 50–75% of the time should be reserved for Essential Standards, with the remainder allocated to Enrichment Standards.

♦ Standards for Continuing Development need not be specifically programmed; they should be built into every appropriate performance task.

♦ Each subject will be governed by approximately 8 to 12 Essential Standards.

♦ Each Essential Standard should have a small number of benchmarks for each grade. Marzano and Kendall (1996) recommend two to four per standard, with an average of three.

♦ Performance tasks take much more time than conventional tests, because they require in-depth problem-solving. According to Marzano and Kendall, teachers they surveyed reported that they could use only 1.5 tasks per month.

Figure 3.2, on the next page, shows how one team developed a comprehensive plan for Grade 5 social studies. Figure 3.2 will be used as an organizer for the explanation that follows.

Using percentages, the team first divided the total time available into three general approaches: Essential Standards to be assessed by performance tasks; Essential Standards to be assessed by conventional tests; and Enrichment Standards, to be assessed as teachers decide. They made this decision by examining several issues: students' developmental maturity; the coverage required by the district's curriculum guide; the total number of standards; and the time they had available to develop performance tasks. They then translated that decision into the number of weeks available for instructional units.

The team then made some rough calculations about the number of units required for each of the three components. They decided that using performance tasks would require more time for each unit; enrichment units could be shorter. By reviewing the curriculum guide, analyzing the standards, and reflecting about their own knowledge of their students, they determined that they would attempt to program their year's work so that they could deal effectively with a total of 17 standards.

Figure 3.2. Planning Matrix for Each Subject

ISSUE	ESS. STD. PERF. TASK	ESS. STD. CON. TEST	ENRICH-MENT STD.	TOTAL
PERCENT TIME	35	35	30	100
WEEKS	13	13	10	36
NO. UNITS	4	6	5	15
NO. STDS	6	6	5	17
NO. BENCH-MARKS	18	18	—	36
PERFORM-ANCE TASKS	4	—	—	4
CONVEN-TIONAL TESTS	—	6	5	11
EMPHASIS	PROBLEM SOLVING	COVERAGE	EXPLOR-ATION	

CODE: ESS. STD. PERF. TASK, Essential Standards to be assessed by performance tasks; ESS. STD. CON. TEST, Essential Standards to be assessed by conventional tests; ENRICHMENT STD., Enrichment Standards.

The next decision was a relatively simple one. They determined that each Essential Standard had an average of three benchmarks and there were no required benchmarks for the Enrichment Standards. After reflecting about the time and resources available, they decided that they could develop four performance tasks for those standards requiring them. They also saw the need for using conventional tests for some of the Essential Standards and for all of the Enrichment Standards.

The "Emphasis" category served as a reminder that each of the three components had a somewhat different emphasis. Those Essential Standards accompanied by performance tasks would emphasize in-depth problem solving. The Essential Standards using conventional tests would enable them to provide the content coverage required by the guide. And the Enrichment Standards would offer all students an opportunity to explore interesting topics that drew upon the teachers' special knowledge and the students' special needs.

Obviously, all these decisions were tentative and revised as the team made progress with its project.

Categorize the Standards

With those decisions made, the instructional team should then review the final list of all the standards and benchmarks produced by the task force. They, again, should consider several factors: their knowledge of their students; their knowledge of the curriculum; state and district tests; textbooks and other resources available. They now assign each standard to one of the three categories: Essential, with performance tasks; Essential, with conventional testing; and Enrichment, with optional assessment.

Develop a Long-Term Plan

The next preliminary step the team should take is to develop a long-term plan that embodies the decisions previously made. For year-long courses, the plan should cover the school year; for courses scheduled for a term, the plan should cover one semester. The form shown in Figure 3.3 has been used successfully by several schools. In the first column are the weeks of the school year in succession. In the second, major events that impact upon teaching and learning are listed

FIGURE 3.3. LONG-TERM PLANNING FORM

TEAM: GRADE 5 SOCIAL STUDIES

DATES	MAJOR EVENTS	UNIT TITLE	STANDARDS	TYPE
9/5–9/9	Opening of school	Before Columbus	Understands native cultures before European explorers	Enrich
9/12–9/16		same	same	same

as reminders; they would include such events as national holidays, seasonal celebrations, and school events. The unit titles are noted next. Then the team indicates the related standards and their type. (A detailed explanation of how to develop long-term plans can be found in Glatthorn, 1994.)

Such a long-term plan has several advantages over daily lesson plans. It helps the teachers conceptualize their planning as whole units, rather than fragmented standalone lessons. It indicates the time allocated to each unit, enabling the team to reflect on its priorities. It shows the progression of units over the long-term. And it links the standards to the units as a means of ensuring that all standards are included in the long-term plan. Once completed by the team, the long-term plan should be reviewed by the principal; it provides an excellent opportunity for dialog between the team and the principal. Some principals have recommended that during the summer teams should develop general plans for the first four weeks of school; then, once they have gotten to know their students better, they can develop plans for the rest of the semester or year.

Teachers who have used these processes have offered several suggestions about this long-term planning process as it relates to the use of performance tasks. First, they suggest that the first performance task should not be presented during the first few weeks of school because those early weeks are needed to establish routines and get to know their students. They also recommend that the performance tasks be spaced over the term or year to ensure that there is ample time between tasks to assemble resources for the next task and to implement enrichment units. If a given classroom performance task is to be used to prepare for state performance assessments, then it should be implemented just prior to the state test. Some teachers prefer to schedule enrichment units at times in the school year when students' interest in school starts to flag, such as the long dry-spell between January and spring break. All these matters can be left to the judgment of experienced teachers.

There are, however, two significant learning issues that planners need to consider. First, they should ensure that the sequence of units helps students see the big picture of the subject and helps students make connections between units. Also, they should keep in mind a very useful recommendation made by Wolf and Reardon (1996): in planning the sequence of units, they should provide for both students and teachers "a developmental frame" for the work. A developmental frame is a carefully structured sequence of units that build upon each other, systematically extending the students' knowledge of that subject and its essential concepts and skills.

DEVELOP THE PERFORMANCE TASK

With this preliminary planning accomplished, the instructional team is ready to develop the first performance task. There is no one right way to do this. The process explained below draws from the extensive literature in the field and the authors' experiences in working with classroom teachers. The process should be implemented flexibly, in a recursive manner. The discussion that follows uses as an example these Grade 5 social studies standard and benchmarks from the Kendall and Marzano (1996, paraphrased from p. 147) compilation:

> STANDARD: Understands institutions of government created during revolution.
>
> BENCHMARKS:
>
> 1. Understands major political issues in 13 colonies.
>
> 2. Understands controversies at Constitutional Convention.
>
> 3. Understands differences between leaders, especially Hamilton and Jefferson.

 ♦ Reflect about the students—their interests, their knowledge, their needs.

The team realizes that their 5th graders probably have no knowledge at all of the forming of the Constitution and are unlikely to be strongly interested in the topic. However, the team also believes that this period is a crucial one in the formation of the nation's governmental system. It believes that interest can be stimulated by referring to the ongoing controversy over federal powers and states' rights.

♦ Reflect about the standard, its benchmarks, and the related learning objectives.

If the objectives have not previously been identified, the team should do so at this time. For example, the first benchmark in the example might be deconstructed into these learning objectives.

- Identifies abolition as key issue.
- Identifies federal and state powers as key issue.
- Identifies separation of powers as key issue.

♦ Reflect about the ways that students might demonstrate their learning.

Thinking about each type of response might stimulate some specific ideas. McTighe and Ferrara (1997) present a very useful typology of performance assessments (paraphrased as follows):

CONSTRUCTED RESPONSES: Short answer; diagrams; visuals (such as a concept map).

PRODUCTS: Essay; research paper and laboratory report; log or journal; story, play, or poem; portfolio; art or science exhibit; model; video- or audiotape; spreadsheet.

PERFORMANCES: Oral report; dance; science demonstration; athletic competition; dramatic reading; enactment; debate; recital.

PROCESSES: Oral questioning; observation; interview; conference; process description; learning log; record of thinking processes.

♦ Consider the purposes of the assessment.

McTighe and Ferrara (1997) suggest these multiple purposes: diagnosis of student strengths and problems; feedback on learning; guidance of instruction; motivation of performance; practice; evaluation or grading; program evaluation.

♦ Brainstorm the performance tasks that might be used.

Suspending critical judgment, team members should do some freewheeling creative thinking, simply listing all the possibilities. Here are some of the ideas that the 5th grade team put on the table.

- Give a speech on either side of one of the issues.
- Publish a newspaper that might have appeared at the time.
- Role play Thomas Jefferson or Alexander Hamilton.
- Make a "You Are There" videotape.
- Write a diary of a representative to the Continental Congress.
- Stage a session of the Continental Congress.
- Write a critique of the Articles of Confederation.

♦ Make a preliminary evaluation of the brainstorming results, and combine ideas or select the one that seems most promising.

At this stage the team should assess the results of the brainstorming. The assessment here should involve two components: a validity check and a reality check. The validity check answers the central question: "Will this performance task enable students to demonstrate that they have acquired the skills and knowledge embodied in the standards and benchmarks?" The reality check answers this question: "Will it work in the classroom?" In making the reality check, you should examine such issues as student interest in the task, the knowledge resources required, the time the task will take, and the teachability of the task. A more systematic evaluation of the performance task occurs later.

Here is the first draft of a performance task that might result from reviewing the brainstorming results in the example:

Pretend that you are a representative from one of the 13 states to the Continental Congress. Present a speech expressing your views on one of the issues and controversies facing that group.

♦ Develop a scenario for the performance task and the assessment-driven instruction.

One useful strategy at this juncture is to develop a scenario for the task and the teaching required. A scenario is a mental picture of how the classroom events unroll—how the class is organized, how the unit starts, how it progresses, and how it ends. The scenario need not be committed to paper; it is simply a planning tool that gives you a clearer picture of how the task and the teaching work together.

Here is the scenario that might be developed for the task listed above:

Organize the class into groups of three—one student per issue. Use the "jigsaw" cooperative learning process to make each student an expert on his or her issue. Each expert returns to his or her group and teaches the others. Each group chooses one of the 13 states that it will represent. The expert from each group makes a speech about the issue he or she knows best. The others in the group help prepare the speech.

Note that the scenario yields a general picture. It is a visioning process that helps you test further the teachability of the task and its accompanying instruction.

♦ Evaluate the first draft of the performance task and revise accordingly.

At this stage a more systematic evaluation by the team is useful. You should find the criteria listed in Figure 3.4, on the next page, helpful in the evaluation process. (These sources were useful in deriving the criteria: Herman, Aschbacher, & Winters, 1992; Wiggins, 1996.)

In the example used here, this initial evaluation would indicate to the developers at least one major deficiency: The performance task as stated did not adequately assess the stud-

FIGURE 3.4. CRITERIA FOR EVALUATING PERFORMANCE TASKS

DOES THE PERFORMANCE TASK

- Correspond closely and comprehensively with the standard and benchmarks it is designed to assess?
- Require the students to access prior knowledge, acquire new knowledge, and use that knowledge in completing the task?
- Require the use of higher thought processes including creative thinking?
- Seem real and purposeful, embedded in a meaningful context that seems authentic?
- Engage the students' interest?
- Require the students to communicate to classmates and others the processes they used and the results they obtained, using multiple response modes?
- Require sustained effort over a significant period of time?
- Provide the student with options?
- Seem feasible in the context of schools and classrooms, not requiring inordinate resources or creating undue controversy?
- Convey a sense of fairness to all, being free of bias?
- Challenge the students, without frustrating them?
- Include criteria and rubrics for evaluating student performance?
- Provide for both group and individual work, with appropriate accountability?

dents' mastery of the benchmark relating to Hamilton and Jefferson. The task would be revised with this addition to the original.

Each individual is also required to write a letter to a friend at home. The letter should report on the progress being made in the Continental Congress, specifically contrasting the leadership of Hamilton and Jefferson.

♦ Develop criteria and rubrics for evaluating student performance.

To accomplish this task, you also need to understand how key terms are being used. (The discussion that follows draws from these sources: Goodrich, 1996; Herman, Aschbacher, & Winters, 1992; and Marzano, Pickering, & McTighe, 1993.)

Criteria are the components of quality that are used as the bases of evaluations. Thus, if you were evaluating a football quarterback, you might use these criteria: pass completion; play-calling ability; avoidance of interceptions; running ability. A *standard* is a statement of expected quality or performance. Thus, a football coach might set this standard for passing accuracy in choosing quarterbacks: "We expect at least a 50% completion rate before we consider any other factors." A *rubric* is a scoring or evaluation tool that lists each criterion and indicates several levels of performance. Figure 3.5, on the next page, shows part of the rubric that would be used in assessing the students' performance of the speech to the Continental Congress. These rubrics would be used to evaluate each student presenting a speech; separate rubrics would be developed for the individual letters.

There are several reasons why you should develop and use criteria and rubrics.

First, they facilitate quality student performance by making clear to the student what is expected. In too many classrooms, students are "flying blind" with no clear knowledge of what constitutes satisfactory performance. In such classrooms teacher feedback is minimal and unclear, using such value language as "try harder," "not your best effort," "not up to my standards." The criteria and rubrics are also useful to the teacher in two ways. First, they provide helpful guidance in preparing and instructing the students. If you have a

FIGURE 3.5. RUBRIC FOR SCORING SPEECHES

CRITERIA/ LEVELS	UNSATISFACTORY	MINIMALLY SATISFACTORY	MORE THAN SATISFACTORY	VERY GOOD	SUPERIOR
GROUP WORK	Does not contribute to group; often disrupts	Makes a few contributions; disrupts occasionally	Makes several contributions, with no disruptions	Makes several useful contributions; facilitates group work	Makes several valuable contributions; provides leadership.
USE OF HISTORICAL KNOWLEDGE					
REASONING ABILITY					
COMMUNICATION SKILL					
OTHER					

clear idea of the criteria, you can give the students the specific help they need in embodying those elements in their perform-ance. They also help the teacher by facilitating the evaluation process, making it fairer, more consistent, and more valid. You can do a better job of grading students if you know the ru-brics. Finally, they help parents understand more clearly what students are being evaluated on and how grades are assigned.

The first step in developing rubrics is to identify the crite-ria to use. Practice has shown that four to seven criteria seem to work best. If there are too few, the feedback is not specific enough. If there are too many, the evaluation process be-comes too complicated. You derive the criteria by answering these related questions: "What factors contribute to overall performance? What do I look for when I evaluate this per-formance?"

Once you have established the criteria, you then decide how many levels of performance to describe. A review of the examples provided in the literature indicates that a range of three to six levels is common. Some experts recommend that you begin by first specifying the two extremes—best and worst—and then filling in the midpoints. (See Goodrich, 1996.)

♦ The next step is to systematize all these decisions
   using a standard format.

Teachers have found that a standard format with three ele-ments is useful: the context; the task; the rubrics. The context identifies the setting—the time and the place—and the stu-dent's role. Here is how the context for the Constitutional Convention task might be presented.

> The year is 1787. The place is Philadelphia. You are
> a representative from one of the 13 original states.
> You are part of a team representing your state at
> the Constitutional Convention. The convention is
> working to establish the basis for the government
> of the new nation. Three issues divide the mem-
> bers. Should slavery be outlawed? Should the
> states or the federal government have more

power? How should the power of the President and the power of the Congress be separated?

Then the task is presented clearly and in specific detail. The students must have a very clear understanding of the problem they are to solve or the performance they are to present. Here is how the task might be specified in the above example.

> You will become an expert on one of these issues. With the help of your team, you will prepare and deliver a speech about that issue to the Convention. Your speech should make clear your team's opinion about the issue. Your speech should last from 10 to 15 minutes. You want to persuade the rest of the Convention members to believe as you do.

You then include the rubrics that have been developed. You also include any individual tasks that you have included to assess each student's mastery. In the example, the each team member would have the individual task of writing a letter about Hamilton and Jefferson.

 ◆ Finally, have the materials evaluated by other professionals and other students.

Because the performance tasks constitute an important part of the instructional and assessment processes, they should be rigorously evaluated by those who have not been involved in developing them. You might ask other teachers, central office supervisors, or university professors to review them. And you should certainly pilot test them with students before they are widely used.

ADMINISTER AND EVALUATE THE RESULTS OF THE PERFORMANCE ASSESSMENTS

The performance tasks have been developed, evaluated, and revised. The final step is to use them to administer the performance assessments, evaluate student performance, and use the results to monitor the achievement cycle.

REFERENCES

Brophy, J., & Alleman, J. (1991). A caveat: Curriculum integration isn't always a good idea. *Educational Leadership, 49* (2), 66.

Bruner, J. (1960). *The process of education.* Cambridge, MA: Harvard University Press.

Gardner, H., & Boix-Mansilla, V. (1994). Teaching for understanding in the disciplines—and beyond. *Teachers College Record, 96,* 198–218.

Glatthorn, A.A. (1994). *Developing the quality curriculum.* Alexandria, VA: Association for Supervision and Curriculum Development.

Goodrich, H. (1996). Understanding rubrics. *Educational Leadership, 54* (4), 14–17.

Herman, J.L., Aschbacher, P.R., & Winters, L. (1992). *A practical guide to alternative assessment.* Alexandria, VA: Association for Supervision and Curriculum Development.

Kendall, J.S., & Marzano, R.J. (1996). *Content knowledge.* Aurora, CO: Mid-continent Regional Educational Laboratory.

Marzano, R.J., & Kendall, J.S. (1996). *A comprehensive guide to designing standards-based districts, schools, and classrooms.* Alexandria, VA: Association for Supervision and Curriculum Development.

Marzano, R.J., Pickering, D., & McTighe, J. (1993). *Assessing student outcomes.* Alexandria, VA: Association for Supervision and Curriculum Development.

McTighe, J., & Ferrara, S. (1997). *Assessing learning in the classroom.* Washington, DC: National Education Association.

Roth, K.J. (1994). Second thoughts about interdisciplinary studies. *American Educator, 18* (1), 44–47.

Vars, G.F. (October, 1991). Integrated curriculum in historical perspective. *Educational Leadership, 49,* (2), 14–15.

Wiggins, G. (1996). Practicing what we preach in designing authentic assessments? *Educational Leadership, 54* (4), 18–25.

Wolf, D.P., & Reardon, S.F. (1996). Can performance-based assessments contribute to the achievement of educational equity? In J.B. Baron & D.P. Wolf (Eds.), *Performance-based student assessment: Challenges and possibilities* (pp. 1–31). Chicago: University of Chicago Press.

4

USING
ASSESSMENT-DRIVEN
INSTRUCTION

At this point you and your colleagues have developed a standards-based curriculum. You have allocated to the several schools the courses for which they will develop performance tasks. You also have produced several planning aids for teachers: a planning matrix for a particular subject; a categorization of the standards in terms of importance and assessment type; a yearly or semester plan showing the sequence of units; and the performance tasks, along with their criteria and rubrics. The next step is to provide teachers with the training they need to develop assessment-based units and to deliver assessment-driven instruction.

This chapter examines one process for developing and implementing assessment-based units. While the process explained here seems to have worked well with many faculties, you and your colleagues should explore other models to find the one best-suited to your needs. (Additional details concerning training and implementation are provided in Chapter 10.)

UNDERSTAND THE IMPORTANCE OF UNIT PLANNING

Planning assessment-based units is an essential step in delivering assessment-driven instruction. As the term implies, an assessment-based unit is a unit that has been carefully planned to prepare students for and engage them in performance assessments so that they might achieve authentic learning.

Several arguments can be advanced for developing units, rather than focusing on single lessons. The unit emphasizes unified and cohesive elements of the curriculum, not fragmented pieces. The unit is broad enough to encompass systematically the skills needed for the performance assessment. The unit shows the students the relationship of parts. The unit is the best structure for organizing problem-solving activities. And the unit provides a solid base for assessment-driven instruction. For these reasons assessment-driven instruction comes out of and is organized by assessment-based units.

ANALYZE THE PERFORMANCE TASK

The first step in the process of developing assessment-based units is to analyze the performance task, keeping in mind the nature of authentic learning. (See Chapter 5 for a full discussion of authentic learning.) To illustrate the ways that such an analysis of the performance task can be made, an example from Grade 6 science will be used. Assume that this is the standard:

> Understand energy sources and their relationship to heat and temperature (paraphrased from Kendall & Marzano, 1996).

Here are the Grade 6 benchmarks derived from that standard:

- Knows that heat is a form of energy
- Defines *heat* and *temperature*, clarifying the distinction
- Explains the relationship of heat and mass
- Explains how heat moves: conduction, convection, radiation
- Knows the sources of heat
- Knows how heat can be conserved, including using insulation

From that standard and those benchmarks, a team of science teachers developed the following performance task (an abbreviated version is presented here as an example):

GROUP TASK: Publish a manual for consumers explaining how they can survive the winter in good shape while conserving heat. Besides giving sound advice, provide supporting scientific evidence derived from your own experimentation.

INDIVIDUAL TASK: Keep a science journal in which you record how your understanding of heat changes throughout the course of this unit; include the results of your own scientific experimentation.

There are two ways to analyze a performance task. One way is to do a *task analysis*, identifying the steps that the learner has to take to accomplish the performance task successfully. In doing a task analysis, you answer this question: "In thinking of my students and their level of development, what steps would they have to take, in sequence, to perform this task?" Here is one sequence for the group task identified above.

♦ Acquire sound and current knowledge about heat conservation and winter survival.

♦ Systematize the new knowledge, organizing it into useful categories: taking care of the person; taking care of the home; taking care of the automobile.

♦ For each suggestion devise and implement a scientific experiment to gather supporting evidence.

♦ Analyze the audience.

♦ Choose an effective format and organization for the manual.

♦ Write the manual, revising with feedback.

The second type of analysis is a *knowledge and skills analysis*. In this analysis, you first determine what knowledge (or declarative knowledge) the students need to accomplish the task; you then determine what skills (or procedural) knowledge they need to master. These are the results of a knowledge/skills analysis for the heat task.

◆ KNOWLEDGE

- relationship of heat and mass
- heat and volume change
- heat and density
- heat and temperature
- sources of heat energy
- heat movement: conduction; convection; radiation
- insulation

◆ SKILLS

- evaluating sources of knowledge
- organizing and storing knowledge
- devising and implementing a scientific experiment to gather evidence
- choosing best format and organization
- writing a consumer manual
- revising

The two methods of analysis yield slightly different results. The results of the task analysis seem more systematic, with an emphasis on skills; the results of the knowledge/skills analysis seem more specific, especially with regard to the knowledge needed. You should experiment with both approaches to determine which works better for you with a given performance task.

BLOCK-IN THE UNIT

The next step in the process is to block-in the unit. The blocking process establishes the general parameters for the unit. These are the decisions you make, with an example from the heat unit:

◆ *Title of the unit:* Surviving the Winter and Saving Heat

◆ *Type of unit:* Assessment-based

♦ *Goal of the unit:* The students will acquire basic knowledge about heat and apply that knowledge to publish a consumer manual.

♦ *Length of the unit:* 3 weeks

You make these decisions by checking the long-term plan, reviewing the results of the analysis, and reflecting again about your students.

REVIEW THE UNIT SCENARIO

As explained earlier, you should develop a unit scenario as a way of testing the feasibility and likely effectiveness of the performance task and the instruction required. The unit scenario is a mental picture of how the unit begins, unfolds, and ends. It is a kind of mental experiment, to see how your plans might work out in practice. You should revisit that scenario with the analysis in mind. Reflect on several issues: the results of your analysis; your students; the standard and its related benchmarks; the performance task; the nature of authentic learning and teaching; the resources available. A scenario for the heat task follows.

> Start by talking about the coming winter and how the students and their families prepare. Learn how much they know. Create a need for the manual. Present the performance task. Begin by establishing the knowledge the whole class needs. Use the videotape on heat. Organize the students into three groups—person, home, auto. Let each group identify a local expert it can interview. Do a short lesson on interviewing techniques. Have each group devise an experiment to test a hypothesis related to its area of research. Bring the students back as a whole class for a lesson on audience analysis. Then let each group write its part of the manual. Arrange for peer editing.

Check your scenario to be sure that it represents authentic learning and reflects the results of the analysis you have made.

SKETCH-IN THE LESSONS

When you are satisfied with the scenario, you should next develop *lesson sketches*. A lesson sketch is a general delineation of what each lesson might include. The goal is not to make detailed lesson plans, but to sketch-in the lessons sufficiently to be sure that the unit can be effectively presented in the time available. There are several forms that lesson sketches can take. One form that many teachers have found effective is shown in Figure 4.1. Down the left side are listed the standard components of an assessment-based unit. Across the top are listed the days of the unit. In Figure 4.1, to conserve space, only the first three days are shown. In actuality the form would show 15 days for a 3-week unit.

FIGURE 4.1. UNIT PLANNING FORM

COMPONENT	DAY 1	DAY 2	DAY 3
ACQUIRE KNOWLEDGE	Activate prior knowledge; View video on heat		
DEVELOP SKILLS		Interviewing	
APPLY KNOWLEDGE, SKILLS IN SOLVING PROBLEM			
DEMON-STRATE LEARNING	Present performance task		
OTHER	Establish need	Set up groups	

A form such as this serves reminds developers of the major components they should include. By examining the form with a horizontal perspective, developers can see how the individual lessons build upon each other and how skills and knowledge are developed. By examining the chart from a vertical perspective, developers can check the lesson plan for a given day.

Another form for the lesson sketch is an outline of the lesson. Here is a written sketch of the first lesson in the heat unit:

- Activate students' prior knowledge by asking them to write briefly in their journals on "All I know about heat." Discuss the results.

- Create interest in the unit by leading a class discussion on how the students and their families prepare for the winter.

- Present the performance task.

- Show the video on heat.

- Check students' understanding of the video's content.

Any form or system that helps you lay out the lessons systematically suffices. Your concern is to make the unit plans specific enough so that you can check their feasibility and likely effectiveness.

PREPARE THE UNIT FOR EVALUATION

Now that you have a general sense of how the unit develops into lessons, you should prepare the unit for evaluation by packaging it for teacher evaluation and use. At this stage especially keep in mind the needs of the teachers who will be using it. You want them to have some flexibility in teaching the unit, while at the same time providing sufficient guidance. Here are the usual components of an assessment-driven unit, in the order of usual presentation.

- Identifying information: School district and address, names of developers, date of publication

- Unit title

- School subject and grade level for intended use

- Suggested number of lessons

- ◆ Curriculum standard and benchmarks the unit addresses
- ◆ Performance task, with criteria and rubrics
- ◆ Lesson sketches (either in chart or written form)
- ◆ Resources required: print, media, software
- ◆ Suggestions for enrichment and remediation
- ◆ Form for evaluating the unit

ARRANGE FOR EVALUATION OF THE UNIT

Each unit should undergo several types of evaluation, using the criteria shown in Figure 4.2, on the next page, or your own set of criteria. First, as you develop and then complete the unit, you and your colleagues should do a formative evaluation, checking periodically to ensure that you are developing quality materials. When you have finished preparing the unit, you should then do a summative evaluation using the same criteria. After making any needed revisions, you should ask teachers who will be using the unit to review and evaluate it, using the criteria and giving you specific suggestions for improving it. You should embody their suggestions in another revision. The real test comes when the students use it. Here the most important criterion is the unit's effectiveness in preparing students to master the performance task. Teachers should supply written feedback on how well the students performed on the task specified.

IMPLEMENT THE ASSESSMENT-BASED UNIT

With the unit developed, the classroom teachers can then implement the unit, checking periodically to ensure that students are developing the skills and knowledge they need to do well on the assessment task. One effective way of keeping an assessment focus is to list on the board the results of the analysis of the performance task. Then, as each lesson concludes, the students can determine with the teacher's guidance what progress was made in that lesson in mastering the required skills and knowledge. The teacher should also check to ensure that authentic learning is taking place, using peer feedback as a check on the teacher's perceptions.

FIGURE 4.2. CRITERIA FOR EVALUATING UNITS

DOES THE UNIT
- Prepare the students to achieve mastery of the performance task?
- Embody the elements of authentic learning?
- Use a realistic time frame?
- In format, organization, and content facilitate teacher use?
- Include all the components specified by the district curriculum office?
- Use language effectively and correctly?

REFERENCES

Brooks, J.G., & Brooks, M.G. (1993). *The case for constructivist classrooms*. Alexandria, VA: Association for Supervision and Curriculum Development.

Kendall, J.S., & Marzano, R.J. (1996). *Content knowledge*. Aurora, CO: Mid-continent Regional Educational Laboratory.

Marzano, R.J., Pickering, D., & McTighe, J. (1993). *Assessing student outcomes*. Alexandria, VA: Association for Supervision and Curriculum Development.

Newmann, F.M., Marks, H.M., Gamoran, A. (1995). *Authentic pedagogy and student achievement*. Madison, WI: Center on Organization and Restructuring of Schools. University of Wisconsin-Madison. ED 389 679.

5

FOSTERING AUTHENTIC LEARNING

If a standards-based curriculum, quality assessments, and assessment-driven instruction are in place, then it is likely that authentic learning will occur.

This chapter provides a closer analysis of the nature of authentic learning and then notes the precautions that are needed if learning is to be maximized.

THE NATURE OF AUTHENTIC LEARNING

Authentic learning is in opposition to standard school learning: authentic learning is the active construction of in-depth knowledge in contextualized problem solving; standard school learning is the acquisition of fragmented, shallow knowledge for the purpose of doing well on examinations. In discussing authentic learning, all teachers should emphasize the mutual responsibility of both the students and the teacher for authentic learning. Figure 5.1, on the next page, shows the learner's responsibilities; Figure 5.2, on page 77, shows the teacher's responsibilities.

Notice that the emphasis is first on learning, not teaching; what the student does is considered the priority issue. While the model in its form here suggests a linear process, it is in reality more recursive and iterative: the learner jumps around, skips steps, and comes back to earlier moves.

THROUGHOUT THE LEARNING EXPERIENCE

Throughout the learning experience, the learners contribute to a supportive classroom environment, keep a focus on

FIGURE 5.1. AUTHENTIC LEARNING:
LEARNER'S RESPONSIBILITIES

♦ Throughout the learning experience
  • I help make the environment one that supports learning.
  • I attend to the learning focus and am motivated to learn.
  • I monitor my own learning, reflect about my learning processes, and am sensitive to my feelings as I learn.
  • I cooperate with the teacher and other learners.
  • I keep in mind the way my performance will be assessed.
  • I value learning: I am aware of feelings and develop positive attitudes towards learning.

♦ I take these steps as I learn
  • I set a meaningful learning goal.
  • I call to mind what I already know, by activating prior knowledge.
  • I acquire new knowledge in depth:
    I organize it.
    I explain it to myself and make my own sense of it.
    I draw pictures and images of it.
    I build it into what I already know, reconceptualizing my knowledge
  • I communicate my new knowledge in elaborated fashion, discussing concepts and sharing ideas.
    I write about it with full details and illustrative examples.
    I draw pictures, diagrams, and schematics representing the knowledge.

I use metaphors and analogies.

- I acquire and apply a learning strategy.
- I use the knowledge and the strategy to work with others in solving a meaningful problem.
- I evaluate my solution.
- I demonstrate and share my knowledge.

FIGURE 5.2. AUTHENTIC LEARNING: TEACHER'S RESPONSIBILITIES

- Throughout the learning experience the teacher
  - Models reflection and insightful thinking and monitors his or her own learning.
  - Helps make the environment one that supports learning.
  - Provides the scaffolding and structure that students need at that time.
  - Helps students work through the steps in the learning experience.
  - Develops and uses performance tasks to assess student learning.
  - Welcomes and uses feedback from students about the teaching/learning experience.
  - Is sensitive to and responds appropriately to the affective dimensionsof learning.

learning, and motivate themselves to accomplish the learning task. They continuously monitor their learning and the processes they are using, cooperate with the teacher and peers, and keep in mind the nature of the performance assessment. They are aware of feelings and work to develop positive attitudes towards the learning process.

THE STEPS IN THE LEARNING PROCESS

Learners, beginning with a meaningful goal, work their way flexibly through a learning process. They activate their prior knowledge. More importantly, they acquire new knowledge in an active processing manner: they organize it with their own strategies, and they construct their own meaning, drawing pictures and images of the new knowledge. A key step is reconceptualizing their prior knowledge in light of new knowledge that they have actively processed.

One of the crucial steps often overlooked in the learning process is communicating the new conceptualization by elaborating on it. The elaborations (providing full written details, giving examples, drawing visual images, and using metaphors and analogies) are ways of representing the knowledge. If students cannot represent their new knowledge, they have not fully understood it.

In the process of solving problems the student probably uses a learning strategy. We define a learning strategy as a sequence of mental operations useful in solving problems. Some strategies are generic, useful in several subjects; for example:

Use a matrix to organize information

Some strategies are subject-specific, such as this one in mathematics:

Identify the known elements of the problem.

The process moves to its conclusion: solving a problem in a social context; evaluating that solution; and communicating and demonstrating that knowledge.

With the learning model clarified, it is then a relatively simple matter, as suggested by Figure 5.2, to identify what the teacher needs to do to make that learning process happen.

The model is neither the best way to teach nor a basis for evaluating teaching. It is, instead, a formulation of a model of learning that captures the central findings of cognitive psychology.

PRECAUTIONS IN USING AUTHENTIC LEARNING

Teachers can misuse authentic learning, with the students learning less as a consequence. The following discussion of precautions in using authentic learning is organized around the principles of authentic learning.

AUTHENTIC LEARNING IS AN INDIVIDUAL MATTER

While certain forms of instruction are described as "individualized," in a true sense, learning always occurs in the individual. As a collection of individuals, groups may show behaviorial change as well, but that change is the sum of individual growth. This first principle, therefore, reminds teachers that even as they appropriately make use of cooperative learning groups, they should be concerned with the achievement of individual students. Slavin (1990) emphasizes the importance of individual accountability when using cooperative learning. Gearhart and Herman (1995) conclude from their research that the quality of student work reflects not only that student's competence but also the amount and quality of assistance received from other students.

Teachers can use several strategies in assessing individual learning when using cooperative learning. First, they can structure group tasks so that each member of the group has a piece of the task to accomplish, relying on peer pressure to ensure that each individual task is accomplished. Second, they can monitor group work closely to observe whether all individuals are actively on task. They can also compute the group score as a sum or average of individual scores, as used in Student Team Learning models of cooperative learning. Finally, they can develop structured systems that enable the members of a cooperative group to evaluate each other's contribution.

AUTHENTIC LEARNING REQUIRES THE ACQUISITION AND USE OF NEW KNOWLEDGE

This principle reminds teachers that authentic learning can take place only when students access new knowledge and use that new knowledge to expand, replace, or deepen existing knowledge. In too many instances, teachers ask students to solve problems simply by brainstorming, without providing a sound knowledge base. Thus, if you ask students to solve a problem of community pollution without adequate scientific knowledge, their solutions are very likely to be flawed.

This principle has several implications for fostering authentic learning. First, identify essential knowledge in the curriculum project, focusing on those central concepts and processes that are vital to understanding that discipline. Second, ensure that assessments require a sound knowledge base. In designing units, structure the unit so that it includes knowledge acquisition. Enable students to access new knowledge, avoiding the teacher lecture as the least effective means. Finally, throughout the unit, monitor students' understanding of the new knowledge.

AUTHENTIC LEARNING REQUIRES REFLECTIVE DIALOG

This principle embodies two closely related components of authentic learning—reflection and discussion. Learning at its best involves reflection about experience—thought that deepens insight. And individual insights need to be tested and shared in group dialog. In too many instances, the class is a busy active place of "buzzing confusion," where reflection is difficult.

One process that seems to work well in fostering reflective insight is this:

♦ Model reflection as you teach, by thinking aloud and emphasizing the importance of reflection.

♦ In class discussions, slow down the pace and increase "wait time." After asking a question, wait at least three seconds before calling on a student or asking for volunteers.

- In examining complex questions, ask the students to reflect individually before using group or class discussion. It helps to have students write their answers to complex questions, because the writing process enables them to bring knowledge to the forefront of consciousness and discern what they know.
- Teach students how to reflect in small groups: taking turns; listening actively; sharing ideas; being open to and resolving constructive differences; learning from and giving to others.

AUTHENTIC LEARNING IS MORE THAN ACTIVITY

Many teachers seem committed to "activity-itis," asking students to engage in activities that are unrelated to the learning goal. For example, teachers who think of themselves as innovative often use role playing as a means of teaching concepts, when it is designed primarily to help the role player empathize with others.

Teachers can apply this principle of authentic learning in several ways. In designing units, emphasize learning outcomes, not activities. In planning individual lessons, ensure that each planned activity relates to the instructional objectives. In teaching lessons, operate flexibly while keeping your sights on the learning goal. And make clear to students the learning purpose of each instructional activity.

AUTHENTIC LEARNING REQUIRES FEEDBACK

All learning requires feedback. The sources can be several: self; the teacher; parents; peers; the computer; external judges; tests. Sometimes the feedback is positive: *right; correct; good work; excellent analysis; objective achieved*. Sometimes it is negative: *wrong; incorrect; not up to standard; poorly phrased; objective not achieved*. Although most teachers seem to avoid giving negative feedback, it can be useful if delivered in an objective and constructive manner. Good and Brophy (1991) note that praise can be counterproductive if it seems manipulative or excessive.

Authentic learning is more likely to take place if the feedback is characterized by these features:

♦ The feedback is timely, delivered as soon as possible after the performance.

♦ The feedback is primarily objective, based upon clear criteria and specific evidence.

♦ The feedback is multiple and from several sources.

♦ The feedback is constructive, emphasizing both the strengths demonstrated and the aspects that can be improved.

AUTHENTIC LEARNING IS AFFECTIVE AND COGNITIVE

The pressure for teacher accountability as measured by test scores seems to have led many teachers to ignore the affective components of the learning experience. However, rather than returning to the 1960s' movement to isolate "affective education," teachers should understand that the affective and the cognitive are closely and perhaps inextricably related to each other. And in many cases the affective element is more important than the cognitive one. Consider, for example, the importance of this affective outcome: enjoy reading. Surely nothing is more significant; yet, that goal is often ignored.

This principle has several implications:

♦ Take time to increase the motivation to learn, emphasizing the meaningfulness of the learning experience.

♦ Be sensitive to students' feelings. Know when to ignore them and when to deal with them.

♦ Take cognizance of the fact that many students have negative attitudes about schooling, testing, and the subjects they study. Acknowledge those attitudes without capitulating to them. Build positive attitudes by making it possible for students to achieve earned success.

♦ Demonstrate positive attitudes yourself and manifest legitimate enthusiasm. Show that you care about the students and value what you are teaching.

♦ Realize that what is learned always goes beyond what is tested. Even the best performance assessments measure only a part of what has been learned. And often the part that is not measured is the most important goal of all, such as:

Develop positive attitudes towards mathematics and enjoy solving mathematical problems as a way of increasing knowledge.

REFERENCES

Gearhart, M., & Herman, J.L. (1995). *Portfolio assessment: Whose work is it? Issues in the use of classroom assignments for accountability.* Los Angeles: Center for the study of Evaluation.

Good, T.L., & Brophy, J.E. (1991). *Looking in classrooms* (5th ed.) New York: HarperCollins.

Slavin, R.E. (1990). *Cooperative learning: Theory, research, and practice.* Englewood Cliffs, NJ: Prentice Hall.

6

USING THE ACHIEVEMENT CYCLE IN SOCIAL STUDIES

Don Bragaw

This chapter explores the development and present status of the achievement cycle in the field of social studies. It presents an historical context for the present standards-movement and a brief appraisal of the various standards that have emerged. Some examples of how assessment-driven instruction can be used in conjunction with such standards are provided by placing such instruction in the perspective of a regard for quality authentic learning.

THE HISTORICAL CONTEXT

In a sense, standards-based curricula and a focus on the test have been alive and well for well over 100 years. The New York State Regents examination, in existence since 1865, has long dictated the currents of both testing and instruction in that state. The examination led, inevitably, to state mandated syllabi, which, focused as they were on only content outlines, dictated extensive content memorization, didactic instructional techniques, and required end-of-the-year state tests. This encouraged teachers to see if they could predict the questions that were to appear on the following year's Regents examination. In the case of social studies (history, geography and political science primarily), if a question requiring knowledge of the Napoleonic domination of European politics was on the previous examination, the chances of its appearing on the following year's test were low. The game of predicting the substance of the examination heavily influenced the curriculum emphasis and the instruction for the year. This was, indeed, assessment-driven instruction, but hardly assessment-driven learning: a major difference between then and now.

Thus, in a very real way did these examinations influence both the curriculum and instruction. For many years, this phenomenon led some colleges and universities, and almost all New York State colleges and universities, to accept Regents examination scores as tantamount to a college entrance examination. In this manner, the university system reinforced the instructional and curriculum pattern for schools, all of whom were primarily geared to the college-oriented student and consistent forms of didactic instruction. The examinations and the syllabi guided teacher and district curriculum and materials choices. It was assumed that the latest college texts would be used. The students would be taught the rigorous process of expository writing in a formulaic manner: state a generalization about the subject (usually a restatement of the question), support the statement with at least two, and preferably three, supporting data, and then end with a concluding statement that succinctly summarizes what had been just written. Three such paragraphs were worthy of the power score of 10–15 points. There were many schools in the state that used these academic standards to make judgments about all students; others made distinctions between Regents and general students. After 1950, recognition was given to what were called non-Regents students, and both the information and writing standards were dropped considerably for those students in an effort to focus on competency regardless of level.

An attempt to alter this process of curriculum design, instructional strategies, and assessment began in the late 1960s with federally sponsored curriculum projects that were concerned with the nature of student critical thought processes—shifting attention to learning and away from memorization, and teacher-dominated classrooms. This emphasis led to greater focus on what Jerome Bruner (1960) identified as the real " process of education"—hands-on student involvement in all aspects of the learning process. History projects, for example, were constructed around the nature of the historical investigation process, not just rote memorization of isolated bits of information. Geography projects involved students in reconciling human demands and geographic limitations through on-site analyses of local problems. Sociologists entered the picture with an emphasis on student activities incorporating actual sociocultural surveys and role playing to emphasize varying perspectives. Similar activities were advocated by political scientists and economists (emphasizing political and economic behavior), and anthropologists (using investigatory tools to study and compare cultures). Identifying real or imagined historical problems, establishing a problem-solving process, and deliberating on alternative solutions—the social scientific thinking process was, in essence, the core of these programs. For their day, these attempts reached few classrooms and impacted on few students. The assessment devices to measure student knowledge remained true and false, multiple choice and fact-based essay questions. As Eisner (1985) pointed out, the emphasis remained on "the effects of such programs on student behavior, with very little attention being paid to the assessment and description of the environment which creates these effects " (p. 6). What these projects had done, however, was to begin the very real examination of the role of critical thinking and problem solving in educational pursuits. Today's leaders of performance assessment were strongly influenced by these attempts to break out of the pattern of rigid, traditional curriculum and didactic instruction. It has taken almost 40 years for the "breakout" to occur in the form of performance assessment procedures that impact on the why and how of learning, not just the what. (Biemer, 1993) Tying all aspects of the learning process together in a meaningful way for students became a focus of the reform of education.

SOCIAL STUDIES STANDARDS

There is now a strong need, at least among leading assessment educators, to have both teachers and administrators use performance assessments to make judgments about the quality of instruction and learning going on in the classroom. This is motivated in no small measure by the various "national" standards issued by the various professional societies' projects. These standards documents profess to establish bottom-line content guides. Some provide benchmarks or indicators of success and some examples of how a student might demonstrate a degree of mastery. Such standards suggest that there is a major difference between possessing information and using the information to demonstrate that intellectual understanding has also occurred. The social studies standards are primarily built around content, such as the following from the *National Standards for United States History*, published by the National Center for History in the Schools (n.d.):

> Standard I: (Students Should Understand:) The characteristics of societies in the Americas, western Europe, and West Africa that increasingly interacted after 1450. (p. 40)

The standard is then subdivided, and further defined by grade level understandings, which, if developmentally implemented would result in greater understanding. Consider this example:

> Standard 1C: (Students should be able to:) Demonstrate understanding of the characteristics of West African societies in the era of European contact by:
>
> > (grade level) 5–12: Describing the physical and cultural geography of West Africa and analyzing its impact on settlement patterns and trade.
> >
> > (grade level) 5–12: Locating the political kingdoms of Mali, Songhai, and Benin, and urban centers such as Timbuktu and Jenne, and analyzing their importance and influence.
> >
> > (grade level) 9–12: Describing how family organization, gender roles, and religion shaped West African societies [Analyze multiple causation]. (1 of 4 grade-level indicators)
> >
> > (grade level) 7–12: Appraising the influence of Islam and Muslim culture on West African societies.

Here is an example of student achievement of Standard 1C at grades 7–12:

Describe the major characteristics of African religious practices and explain how they affected child-
rearing practices such as naming ceremonies and
age groupings; the role of the individual and social
relationships; and attitudes toward nature and use
of the land. (1 of 3 grade-level examples)

The method by which an individual teacher would help
students reach the standard is entirely optional with the
teacher. While this example is fairly typical of the format of
the other social science standards, the social studies community has either accepted or rejected them. There also has been
criticism of the history standards by conservative critics, who
were dismayed by inadequate mention of such historical figures as Paul Revere and an overemphasis on multiculturalism. The geography standards have received a warmer reception because they have combined content with process to a
much greater extent. They are also limited to a manageable
number, and are less prone to patriotic assertions. The Civics
standards, while based on political science research, are also
fewer in number, but still consist of a similar schema (Center
for Civic Education, 1994). It has been far more difficult for
the social scientists to control the demands of various constituencies for content inclusion, than some of the other academic areas such as mathematics and English. In the field of
history, the standards projects have to face the additional
daunting task of reconciling conflicting claims to knowing
what is best for children.

UNITING STANDARDS AND ASSESSMENTS TO GUIDE INSTRUCTION IN GEOGRAPHY

What is that process, and what are the assessment tools,
by which such learning can presumably occur in social studies? In the introductory chapters of this volume, a suggested
organizational pattern (Figure 1.3, p. 13) was presented. The
following example from geography shows how the process
might work.

ASSUMPTIONS:

♦ A district task force has been convened, and has issued a set of guiding principles.

♦ The final report recognizes that the standard indicated below is essential to the district's emphasis on geography:

> Standard Three: How to analyze the spatial organization of people, places and environments on the earth's surface.

By the end of the 12th grade level, the national geography standards assert that the student should know and understand:

♦ The generalizations that describe and explain spatial interaction.

♦ The models that describe patterns of spatial organization.

♦ The spatial behavior of people.

♦ How to apply concepts and models of spatial organization to make decisions.

(National Geographic Research and Exploration, 1994, pp. 188–189)

In simple terms, what this standard calls for is the student's understanding of how people have utilized space on the earth's surface. An example of this idea for rural or suburban students might be the study of the decisions concerning the location of a shopping mall or a housing development in an area adjoining farms. For urban students, the tearing down of a row of deserted houses and the rise of new apartments or shopping areas may be relevant. Student acquaintance with rural, suburban, or urban settings in other cultures may not be part of their experience and some basic geography will need to be introduced, but the concepts remain the same. The increasingly important issue of local annexation of adjoining territory into an incorporated village or city because of population expansion, may not be a prominent issue in a student's life. When, however, students are confronted with the reassignment of themselves or their friends to other schools because of the annexation, it becomes a real issue. The spatial relationships are much more obvious and provide a firm base upon which to center instruction. The transference of such learning to the displacements of people due to war conditions (in Bosnia or central Africa), may now become more understandable. Flooding by many major rivers demonstrates the interaction of people with the natural processes of the earth. Is it wise to settle on lowland adjoining a major river subject to great variations in the volume of water being channeled? Are insurance companies correct in refusing to insure houses in a flood plain unless residents take steps to provide for greater flood security? The multiple contemporary and historical examples of the interaction of people and geography in the uses of space are almost limitless: hurricanes along the southeastern U.S. coast; monsoon or cyclonic conditions in India or Bangladesh; building of dams to irrigate desert areas; disputes over the disposal of nuclear waste.

Critical to the examination, however, is the students' increasing ability to apply these lessons to their own lives. Will students become more aware of zoning issues if they are actively engaged in examining the annexation and reassignment issues through a performance oriented instructional experience? Will the destruction of the world's rainforests, the location of nuclear waste disposal areas, or the location of hog farms and disposal of hog waste have any greater meaning when students are confronted by these issues in their lifetimes?

These developments will occur if teachers engage the students in examining the issues in real terms. What is the problem? What are the multiple objectives involved? Teachers need to help students decide on activities that are real and relevant to the goals, such as researching the population explosion; interviewing zoning officials about the nature of political, economic, geographic, and school zoning patterns; participating in surveys of people living in affected areas; observing and participating in local governance hearings on the issue; examining the present zoning and land use policies and maps. Of course, such study would have even greater meaning if it were done before the final decisions of the town council, and the students were given an opportunity to offer a recommendation to that council. There are many such local issues in which the spatial standard is a key understanding. Each of the steps involved in the annexation issue might, for example, become part of a team and/or individual student portfolio with each portfolio item revealing the types and kinds of activities and the quality of performance of the individual student. The student is judged by the breadth and depth of his or her progress, having participated in establishing the criteria for such judgment in the initial phases of the project. (See Kon and Martin-Kneip, 1992, for other examples)

This, of course, is an example of a "performance assessment" that has greater meaning because it directly involves the students in a student-relevant occasion thus fulfilling the Newmann (Newmann and associates, 1996) criteria of authentic learning. However, as the introductory chapters indicate, the performance task and assessment can be done in a more modest way and be accomplished in a self-contained classroom setting. The teacher could attain many of the same standards goals by using aerial maps of the area under study. This would be in the form of actual maps, overheads, or computer-enhanced photographs. Teams of students might be given specific tasks which will point up the spatial considerations needed for decision making: for example, where would they locate an additional shopping mall? A combined golf course–housing project? A hog farm? A nuclear waste plant? A new school? Or, as related to the above annexation issue, how would they justify a student population relocation plan of their own?

Each of the teams would be asked to make an oral, visual and written presentation explaining both the where and the why of their recommended site locations. They would need to be clearly knowledgeable about geographic and human considerations and subject themselves to criticism from their peers, defending their position where necessary. The teacher's role is multiple: provide needed instruction in helping students identify a problem; establish reasonable goals and the criteria by which goal-fulfillment is to be gauged; guide students in their research efforts, involve them in planning appropriate activities and monitor their progress. This assessment-driven instruction would have three evaluation sources all based on the previously established criteria: the students' evaluations of their individual or group performance, their peers' critique, and a teacher judgment about their contribution to the entire process.

The key question is: Did the students clearly demonstrate a knowledge of the relationship between space and human interaction with that space according to the criteria established at the onset of the project? A true indicator of student understanding would be if, when given several different problems, they could transfer their real knowledge about space and human interaction. For example, could they more easily understand the vast human, political, economic, and cultural dimensions of the new settlement in and destruction of the Brazilian rainforest? Can they see such relationships between President Jackson's decision to "remove" the Cherokee people from their homes in North Carolina and the accommodation of the advancing white settlements on the available land? Can they better understand the political practice of "gerrymandering," or take action when hearing of restrictive real estate zoning practices in their local county? The value of establishing standards at all major levels of the curriculum is that the standard, if it is worthy, expands with successive exposure to related issues, although dealing with a wide variety of content over the course of a student's school experience. Assessment-driven instruction may carry with it an important message: that knowledge and action are integral parts of examining a problem (Parker, 1990) Again, the Newmann criteria for authentic achievement and learning are met, and the instructional base of the student involvement is away from teacher dominance. The activity itself, if properly framed and organized, fosters all of the positive gains to be achieved from assessment-driven instruction.

NATIONAL HISTORY STANDARDS AND PERFORMANCE ASSESSMENT

Another example might be derived from the National History Standards (National Center for History in the Schools, n.d.). While these standards are still somewhat controversial, most of them are realistic and achievable. Consider, for example, the standard which reads:

> (Students should be able to:) Demonstrate understanding of the New Frontier and Great Society and analyze their domestic accomplishments.

The standard requires the students not only to know information about these two programs of Presidents Kennedy and Johnson, but to be able to indicate whether these domestic programs were successful or not. This may well establish the foundation for a major debate: teams would be formed for defending or denying the effectiveness of these two programs. The teacher and students would develop a list of criteria for accomplishing this debate task. Such criteria might include:

- ◆ Do students possess accurate and sufficient information to support their position?
- ◆ What criteria will be used to measure "accomplishments"?
- ◆ Have the teams made appropriate applications of their new knowledge to present day programs?
- ◆ Are debaters fully aware of debate procedures and courtesies?

If the debate format and criteria are fully spelled out at the beginning of the exercise, the students would need to frame research questions, conduct the research (both individually and as a team), pursue discussions as to the accomplishments, make necessary adjustments in their research if necessary, and then organize their presentation. Team, class, and teacher assessment of the value of the presentation would determine how well each group performed. (See also Kobrin, et al., 1990.)

SYNTHESIZING STANDARDS AND PERFORMANCE IN SOCIAL STUDIES

A more encompassing set of standards is provided by the National Council for the Social Studies (1994). Because the nature of social studies is so diverse, the National Council took it upon itself to try to synthesize the social sciences and give teachers umbrella standards that utilized the various individual social science content standards. The way in which this was accomplished was by providing a framework of ten unifying themes: culture; time, continuity, and change; people, places and environments; individual development and identity; individuals, groups, and institutions; power, authority, and governance; production, distribution, and consumption; science, technology, and society; global connections; and civic ideals and practices. While one or another of these themes might well center on history or economics, the themes are intended to be interdisciplinary. Thus, the study of culture cannot be accomplished by studying history alone, but must include data from all of the social sciences. The study of civic ideals and practices is not confined to political science, for civic ideals are frequently the product of culture, historical precedent, or geographic location, as well as other influences. It is clear as well that the social studies recognizes and incorporates data from sources outside the social sciences to enhance student understanding. The most positive feature of these standards is that they recognize that teachers can use a wide spectrum of information from the various social and other sciences to implement the standard.

This is an example of one of the National Council's standards:

> Social Studies programs should include experiences that provide for the study of people, places, and environments. (p. 23)

This standard could easily incorporate geography and history standards. For example, Students should be able to:

> Demonstrate understanding of transformations in Europe following the economic and demographic crises of the 14th Century, by....

(National Center for History in the Schools, n.d., p. 156.) The National Council then provides specific performance expectations (K-12) such as these for high school students:

> Social Studies programs should include experiences that provide for the study of people, places and environments, so that the learner can (selected items, p. 118)
>
> • refine mental maps of locales, regions, and the world that demonstrate understanding of relative location, direction, size, and shape.
>
> • describe, differentiate, and explain the relationships among various regional global patterns of geographic phenomena such as land forms, soils, climate, vegetation, natural resources, and population.
>
> • describe and assess ways that historical events have been influenced by, and have influenced, physical and human geographic factors in local, regional, and global settings.
>
> • propose, compare, and evaluate alternative policies for the use of land and other resources in communities, regions, nations, and the world.

Clearly, the assessment-driven examples concerning President Jackson's removal of the Cherokee Indians, location of nuclear sites, and the realignment of school district boundaries, are appropriate topics and activities to carry out the standard. The Council also provides specific examples, or classroom case studies, of how these standards might be practiced in the classroom. Just one example suggests the flavor of the whole document:

> The problem presented to Nancy Gilligan's civics class is: Where will the new landfill be located? The students have been studying how national issues and problems affect local communities. Now they have undertaken the task of finding solutions to a real community problem.

> The students, working in small groups, are required to develop a set of criteria for examining potential landfill sites, determine the location of at least two available sites in their community, and assess those locations against their criteria. Each group presents arguments to support its decision to locate the landfill in a particular area. Such items as charts, videos, taped interviews with affected residents, and environmental impact projections are packaged into a multimedia production for class review and evaluation.
>
> The group presentations are assessed on: strength of criteria used to make the decision; persuasiveness of presentation; accuracy and appropriateness of supporting data, and overall quality of the presentation. (pp. 118–119)

Are the tasks described in the three cited examples classroom-friendly? Are they "doable" in terms of accomplishing the multiple aims of education: the acquisition of content knowledge; the development of useful life skills; the acquisition of research processes; the maturation of intellectual curiosity; and the enhancement of dispositions toward lifelong learning? Several questions might test it:

- ◆ Would it achieve the goal of student accomplishment of the established standard?
- ◆ Would it be possible to establish an acceptable assessment rubric by which the student work can be evaluated?
- ◆ Would it satisfy the goal of active, constructivist, student learning?
- ◆ Would the teacher be able to monitor the entire process with a fair amount of confidence that student involvement would decrease student ennui or misbehavior?

This process would not necessarily obviate the need for further checks on student knowledge of specific terminology or procedures. This caution should be made clear from the beginning. A knowledgeable person is able to communicate using the correct terminology, conveying the process in oral or written language; but the teacher needs to make the judgment as to how and when such knowledge is to be acquired or demonstrated.

SUMMARY: USING CURRICULUM STANDARDS IN SOCIAL STUDIES

Figure 6.1 summarizes the status of curriculum standards in social studies and offers recommendations to school systems interested in developing standards-based curricula. Those recommendations represent the considered judgment of this author and should be reviewed critically by local developers.

FIGURE 6.1. SUMMARY: CURRICULUM STANDARDS IN SOCIAL STUDIES

Primary sources

Kendall, J.S., & Marzano, R.J. (1996). *Content knowledge.* Aurora, CO: Mid-continent Regional Educational Laboratory.

National Council for the Social Studies. (1994). *Curriculum standards for social studies: Expectations of excellence.* Washington, DC: Author.

Strands used

The NCSS report identifies ten recurring themes, which can be used as curriculum strands. Kendall and Marzano organize the standards by specific subjects, as follows: history; geography; civics; economics; behavioral studies (sociology, psychology, and social anthropology). The Kendall/Marzano strands are adapted from those developed by the various professional organizations.

Subject organization

No specific subject organization is recommended in either document. Kendall and Marzano identify grade-level benchmarks for each of the subjects specified. The themes identified by the NCSS report are intended to be interdisciplinary, drawing content from the several subjects usually taught under the umbrella of "social studies." The ten themes are as follows: culture; time, continuity, and change; people, places, and environments; individual development and identity; individuals, groups, and institutions; power, authority, and governance; production, distribution, and consumption; science, technology, and society; global connections; and civic ideals and practices.

Summary of standards

The Kendall/Marzano compilation seems to include an excessive number of standards. Also, the standards identified seem to emphasize content or declarative knowledge, with less concern for process or procedural knowledge. The NCSS standards, on the other hand, are general statements that seem to provide a more balanced inclusion of content and process. The NCSS report also provides performance expectations for each theme, along with specific examples.

Recommendations to school districts

- ◆ Where state standards exist and are of satisfactory quality, use state standards as the foundation.
- ◆ Determine optimal subject emphasis, grade by grade.
- ◆ Use the NCSS standards to add to the state standards or to provide a foundation if state standards do not exist or lack sufficient specificity.
- ◆ Use the strands identified by the NCSS document.
- ◆ Check the resulting document against the recommendations of subject-focused professional groups.

A CONCLUDING NOTE

Performance assessment in social studies has the same implications as in other areas of the curriculum; the change that is necessary for assessment-driven instruction to work is to change the mind-set of administrators, teachers and parents, so that they avoid what Grant Wiggins (1989) once called "The Futility of Trying to Teach Everything of Importance." Some very real evaluation of what it is that students should know and understand must be made if the social studies in schools is to be reality based, and authentically achieved. History is not an avalanche of names, dates, and discordant facts, but the story of a very exciting human adventure—but the Albigensian Crusade is not a crucial part of that story. Geography is not just maps and globes, latitudes and longitudes, but the very real interaction of people with their natural and cultural surroundings. Political science or civics is a decision-making and policy forming enterprise, not a terminological jungle. For administrators and teachers the byword in social studies is "letting go": letting go of the traditional views of transmitting too much information and beginning the active process of helping students use information to develop understanding—sometimes with computer assistance. Assessment-driven instruction can lead to that goal.

This "letting go" process has been severely complicated by the proliferation of "academic standards" propounded by each of the professional social science associations, or their agents, all eager to get on the standards "bandwagon" and assert the dominance of their own discipline. (Grant, 1995) This has once again called attention to the need in the social studies for a "centering" process—a synthesizing effort that would enable schools to begin to address a realistic body of achievable knowledge based on the social science standards. The situation calls for the application of the "performance assessment" concept to both administrative and teacher decisions about what should be included, or excluded, in the social studies curriculum. A clear rubric of established criteria—not unlike that established for student performance—is just as important if students are not to be buried in an avalanche of information.

REFERENCES

Biemer, L. (1993). Trends in social studies: authentic assessment. *Educational Leadership, 50*(8) 81.

Bruner, J. (1960). *The process of education.* Cambridge, MA: Harvard University Press.

Center for Civic Education. (1994). *National standards for civics and government.* Calabasas, CA: Author.

Eisner, E.W. (1985). *The art of educational evaluation.* London: Falmer Press.

Grant, S.G. (1995). Nightmares and possibilities: a perspective on standard-setting. *Social Education, 59,* 443.

Kobrin, D., Abbott, E., Ellinwood, J., & Horton, D. (1990). Learning history by doing history. *Educational Leadership, 50* (7), 39–41.

Kon, J.H., & Martin-Kneip, G.O. (1992). Students' geographic knowledge and skills in different kinds of tests: multiple-choice versus performance assessment. *Social Education. 56,* 95–98.

National Center for History in the Schools. (n.d.). *National standards for world history.* Los Angeles: Author.

National Council for the Social Studies. (1994). *Curriculum standards for social studies: Expectations of excellence.* Washington, DC: Author.

National Geographic Research and Exploration. (1994) *Geography for life. National geography standards.* Washington, DC: Author.

Newmann, F.M., and associates. (1996). *Authentic achievement: restructuring for intellectual quality.* San Francisco: Jossey-Bass Publishers.

Parker, W.C. (1990). Assessing citizenship. *Social Education, 48* (3), 17–22.

Wiggins, G. (1989). The futility of trying to teach everything of importance. *Educational Leadership, 46* (3) 44–59.

7

USING THE ACHIEVEMENT CYCLE IN SCIENCE

Karen Dawkins

Although performance tests have long been a component of assessment in science classes, they have not necessarily incorporated the criteria specified in this book. In fact, the phrase "performance assessment" as used in science education has been applied to almost any type of test that involves the manipulation of materials to indicate understanding at some level (Brown & Shavelson, 1996; Carter and Berenson, 1996; Tamir, 1985). This chapter deals with performance assessments in a broader context, including any type of task that illustrates a student's ability to apply knowledge. Examples include not only materials-based laboratory tasks, but also writing assessments such as journal writing and open-ended problems, portfolio assessments, interview assessments, and classroom presentations.

This chapter discusses ways to develop science standards, design performance assessments, and use assessment-driven instruction in classrooms.

DEVELOPING STANDARDS IN SCIENCE

The following section suggests how the subject task force for science might incorporate national, state, and local priorities in writing standards for a quality program of science education. There are several documents that are useful resources for defining standards. In using these sources, however, it is important to remember a point made earlier: focus on depth rather than breadth. Ahlgren (1996) warns that one of the greatest dangers in curriculum development is the temptation to ignore the hard won consensus among science educators that the amount of content should be reduced. It is easy to include most of the current content and simply to resort it to fit standards.

DECIDE ON A BASIS FOR CURRICULUM ORGANIZATION

What students should learn and how they should learn it are philosophical considerations that have changed over the years, affecting the principles underlying science curricula. According to Bybee and DeBoer (1994), in the last century, goals of science education have ranged from a means of disciplining the mind, to applying problem-solving to the social ills early in this century, to a focus on national security during the Cold War era. More recently, issues such as the environment, infectious diseases, and birth control have stimulated an interest in the societal applications of science. Concern about our competitiveness in world markets has prompted a focus on science education as a means of insuring national economic security.

Traditionally, standards in K-12 science education have been organized under the strands of the science disciplines—life sciences, earth/space sciences, and physical sciences (chemistry and physics)—but those are not the only organizational schemes advocated by science educators as a part of contemporary reform. Citing the appeal to a larger segment of the student population, Hofstein and Yager (1982) argued that the basis for organizing science curriculum should be social issues rather than the traditional scientific disciplines. Arguing against the science and society theme, Good, Herron, Lawson, and Renner (1985) suggested that science education was "the discipline devoted to discovering, developing, and evaluating improved methods and materials to teach science, i.e., the quest for knowledge, as well as the knowledge generated by that quest" (p. 140).

The National Science Teachers Association (1992), the American Association for the Advancement of Science (1990, 1993), the National Research Council (1996), and Kendall and Marzano (1996) use traditional science disciplines as a basis for organizing curriculum, but they also emphasize social relevance as well as the history and nature of science, and science as inquiry.

DECIDE ON THE RELATIONSHIP OF KNOWLEDGE AND SKILLS

A major challenge to organizations attempting to define content standards in science has been the difficulty of managing a body of knowledge that is expanding exponentially. Two extreme positions are sometimes advocated. Some argue that teachers should ignore the base of scientific knowledge and focus entirely on scientific skills such as observing, inquiring, and experimenting; others believe that teachers should teach students as many facts about the workings of the physical universe as possible. A moderate view is espoused by the National Science Teachers Association (1992), the American Association for the Advancement of Science (1990, 1993), and the National Research Council (1996). Their perspective advocates the involvement of students in scientific inquiry set in the context of current scientific knowledge, thereby integrating content knowledge with the skills used by practicing scientists to generate that knowledge.

DECIDE ON STRANDS AND STANDARDS

The *National Science Education Standards* (National Research Council, 1996) uses eight categories which span K-12, but under those categories, each standard appears only once at one grade-span (K-4, 5–8, or 9–12). For example, there is no standard within the physical science category which crosses all grade spans to be articulated at one level for primary students and at another level for middle graders or high school students. There are related standards, however, which might be restated in more general terms appropriate for the entire K-12 continuum. For example, within the physical science strand, standards are based on these topics (p. 106):

K-4: Properties of objects and materials

5–8: Properties and changes of properties in matter

9–12: Structure and properties of matter

Kendall and Marzano consolidate those ideas into a single standard: "Understands basic concepts about the structure and properties of matter" (p. 92).

Because of the intensity of research and development activity related to the reform movement in science education in recent years, there are numerous helpful publications that might provide a strong foundation for defining strands and standards appropriate for your local school system. In addition to the sources mentioned previously, nearly every state's Department of Education has a framework or curriculum document of some type for K-12 science education.

DECIDE ABOUT SPECIFIC BENCHMARKS FOR EACH STANDARD

Science content standards, clustered under traditional science discipline strands, provide a logical foundation for the development of specific benchmarks. For example, the physical science standard defined by Kendall and Marzano covers benchmarks appropriate for each grade span. Examples include:

Grades K-2: "Knows that objects can be described and classified by their composition (wood, metal) and their physical properties (color, size, shape)" (pp. 92–93).

Grades 3–5: "Knows that things have properties (e.g., magnetism, conductivity, density, solubility) that can be used to tell them apart and to find out which of them are alike" (p. 93).

Grades 6–8: "Knows that there are more than 100 known elements that combine in numerous ways to produce compounds, which account for the living and nonliving substances that we encounter; chemical elements do not break down by normal laboratory reactions such as heating, electric current, or reaction with acids" (p. 93).

Grades 9–12: "Knows that an element is composed of a single type of atom; when elements are listed in order according to the number of protons (called the atomic number), repeating patterns of physical and chemical properties identify families of elements with similar properties..." (p. 94).

ANALYZE THE BENCHMARKS

Using the sources cited earlier, develop a comprehensive list of benchmarks and determine how they will fit into your organizational scheme.

MASTERY BENCHMARKS

Because a comprehensive science curriculum includes standards for science content knowledge as well as skills involved in doing science, it is helpful to differentiate between knowledge and skills in order to develop appropriate benchmarks. For example, the publications mentioned earlier, as well as most state curriculum documents, give attention to process skills, science inquiry methods, and manipulation of scientific equipment and materials. Consider developing mastery benchmarks for the content standards in each of the science discipline standards and perhaps treating the skills differently.

INCORPORATED SKILLS

Among the important considerations in a K-12 curriculum are the standards for skills best addressed in the context of the science knowledge base. The National Research Council (1996) reiterates the following standard at each grade span: "All students should develop abilities to do scientific inquiry" (p. 173). It is much more meaningful to address these skills as students are exploring the scientific body of knowledge. For example, when sixth graders are learning the differences between acids and bases, they can learn how to design and implement an experiment to test household products for acid/base content.

ENRICHMENT BENCHMARKS

You will identify more benchmarks in the publications you read than you can reasonably expect to address. Adhering to the honored principle that "less is more," specify as enrichment benchmarks those specific knowledge and skills to be introduced only after students successfully reach the mastery benchmarks.

ADD ANY NEEDED MASTERY BENCHMARKS

If your state or district administers end-of-year tests, examine the content and skills on which the tests are based. If there are any areas not addressed at appropriate grade levels in your set of benchmarks, make the adjustments as needed.

In science, there are often special areas of interest in a particular geographical area, and teachers might wish to add mastery benchmarks that address those local concerns. Students living on the Outer Banks of North Carolina could study the unique geological processes at work on barrier islands while the schools in isolated Alaskan villages might emphasize benchmarks related to plant and animal adaptations in harsh environments.

SUMMARY: CURRICULUM STANDARDS IN SCIENCE

Figure 7.1 summarizes the status of curriculum standards in science and recommends how school systems might best use them in developing standards-based curricula.

FIGURE 7.1. SUMMARY: CURRICULUM STANDARDS IN SCIENCE

Primary sources

American Association for the Advancement of Science. (1993). *Benchmarks for science literacy.* New York: Oxford University Press.

National Research Council. (1996). *National science education standards.* Washington, DC: National Academy Press.

Strands used

The AAAS document identifies no strands as such, but specifies common themes: systems, models, constancy and change, and scale. The standards document from NRC identifies five unifying concepts and processes that might be considered strands. They include the following: systems, order, and organization; evidence, models, and explanation; constancy, change, and measurement; evolution and equilibrium; and form and function.

Subject organization

Neither document specifies a subject sequence. The NRC standards, however, do include three subject-specific categories: physical science; life science; and earth/space science. At the high school level these translate logically into traditional high school science courses.

Summary of standards

The AAAS publication does not identify standards; rather, it identifies benchmarks for grade ranges clustered under the general areas of science, mathematics, and technology. In the first 11 chapters, all benchmarks are related to content—what students should know. The final chapter ("Habits of Mind") addresses skills in these areas: computation and estimation; manipulation and observation; communication skills; and critical response skills.

The NRC report includes standards addressing both content and skills. In addition to the three standards focusing on the traditional science subjects, standards address these areas: unifying concepts and processes; science as inquiry; science and technology; science in personal and social perspectives; history and nature of science. Standards that target skills are clustered in two of the categories—science as inquiry and science and technology.

Recommendations to school districts

- ◆ If state standards are philosophically consistent with national standards, use state standards as an organizational tool.
- ◆ Determine subject emphases for secondary grades.
- ◆ Because state standards are often minimal requirements, use the NRC standards and the AAAS benchmarks to develop a fuller and richer foundation for curriculum development.

DESIGNING PERFORMANCE ASSESSMENTS

Refer to Chapter 3 for the iterative process used to develop rich performance assessments. In science, there are certain standards and related benchmarks that lend themselves to performance assessments. They include standards related to scientific inquiry skills, standards related to the nature and history of science, and standards that have obvious applications in real-world situations.

STANDARDS RELATED TO SCIENTIFIC INQUIRY SKILLS

Performance tasks are particularly useful methods to assess students' proficiency in the practice of scientific inquiry, including process skills, manipulation of scientific equipment, and proper use of laboratory safety equipment. Those assessments may measure single skills or multiple skills, depending on the complexity of the task, and they may or may not be set in the context of a science content area (physics, biology, chemistry, earth/space science). The examples that follow assess at least two benchmarks each, related to either the same standard or to two or more standards.

SCIENCE STANDARD: Develop abilities to do scientific inquiry.

Grade 6 benchmarks: (1) Identify questions that can be answered through scientific investigations; and (2) design and conduct a scientific investigation.

SCIENCE STANDARD: Understand basic concepts about the structure and properties of matter.

Grade 6 benchmark: Know that materials have different states (solid, liquid, gas), and some common materials such as water can be changed from one state to another by heating or cooling.

Assessment Task: Design an experiment that compares the phase changes of two materials. Include these steps in your design:

1. Choose two materials that are the same phase at room temperature (materials that are safe for you to use).

2. Pose a question that you want to answer about the comparison.

3. Use the library to research the properties of the two materials and, from your findings, state a hypothesis.

4. Design an experiment to test your hypothesis, including a materials list and safety precautions.

5. Write your experimental design using the following headings: question, hypothesis, materials, procedures, safety precautions.

This task involves only the written experimental design. If the experiment can be safely and practically performed by students, a second assessment task might involve a comparison of experimental results among groups as well as a comparison of class findings with findings of professional scientists.

STANDARDS RELATED TO THE HISTORY AND NATURE OF SCIENCE

The research indicates widespread misconceptions about the nature of science among teachers and students (Duschl, 1994; Lederman, 1992). According to Arons (1988), Bentley and Garrison (1991), and Wandersee (1985), an effective strategy for teaching about the nature of science is in the context of science content topics through historical cases. Major theories in each scientific discipline provide rich cases of scientists and their work: atomic theory (chemistry), theory of plate tectonics (geology), theory of planetary motion (physics), and cell theory (biology). The following assessment task uses this strategy in the context of organ systems in biology.

SCIENCE STANDARD: Understands the nature of scientific knowledge.

High School Benchmarks (from Kendall and Mar-zano): (1) Knows that science distinguishes it-self from other ways of knowing and from other bodies of knowledge through the use of empirical standards; and (2) knows that scien-tific explanations must meet certain criteria; they must be consistent with experimental and observational evidence about nature; and they must include a logical structure, rules of evi-dence, openness to criticism, reporting meth-ods and procedures, and a commitment to mak-ing knowledge public.

SCIENCE STANDARD: Knows the general struc-ture and function of cells in organisms.

High School Benchmark: Understands the struc-ture and function of systems in animals.

Assessment Task: You will work in groups of four to develop a historical vignette based on your re-search into the life and work of a scientist chosen from the list you have been given. Each of these sci-entists has contributed to the scientific knowledge base regarding the respiratory and circulatory sys-tems of animals (including humans). Your assign-ment is detailed below:

1. Choose a scientist from the list provided.

2. Research the life and work of your scientist in the library.

3. From the information you gather, write a script for your group to use in a five-minute dramatic presentation for the class (with appro-priate costumes and props). You may present your vignette live or prepare a videotape. Con-sider the following questions in your research: (a) What did the scientist contribute to the knowledge base about circulatory/respiratory systems? (b) What ideas did he refute (if any)? (c) Which part of his work was replication of

studies done by other scientists (if any)? (d) What theories did his work support (if any)? (e) How did his scientific peers and the general public receive his findings? (f) What part of his work has been replaced by more modern ideas?

4. Individual assignment: After all the presentations have been made, choose a scientist portrayed by another group and write a two-page comparison of that scientist's views with those of your scientist, citing the evidence used by each to support those views. Include a paragraph stating your opinion about the strength of the evidence presented and the logic of the conclusions drawn by each scientist.

STANDARDS WITH REAL-WORLD APPLICATIONS

Standards that deal with the environment or with research topics in the news offer rich opportunities for students to develop real-world applications. Related assessment tasks give students a chance to make connections, and thus to make sense of scientific knowledge in the context of their lives.

SCIENCE STANDARD: Understands the interactions of science, technology, and society.

Grade 3 Benchmark: Develops understanding of science and technology in local challenges.

Grade 3 Benchmark: Implements proposed solutions using suitable tools, techniques, and quantitative measurements where appropriate.

Assessment Task: After reading the story of *The Magic School Bus at the Waterworks* (Cole, 1986), pretend that you are a water quality technician at the waterworks. Choose the appropriate measuring instrument from your station to measure 50 milliliters of water from the pan of dirty water at the supply station. Draw a picture of your measuring instrument showing the dirty water inside and the marks that indicate that you have 50 milliliters.

Choose any equipment from the supply station that you think will enable you to clean the dirt from the water. Try to clean your water. Draw a picture showing how you set up your equipment. Write a few sentences telling how your experiment worked. If it did not work as well as you wish, write about that and choose other materials for a second try.

USING ASSESSMENT-DRIVEN INSTRUCTION

A major advantage of carefully defining standards and benchmarks and then constructing related assessment tasks is to focus instruction on the learning goals deemed most important by teachers and school leaders. The following section offers suggestions for instructional strategies that support standards related to scientific inquiry skills, standards related to the nature and history of science, and standards that have real-world applications.

TEACHING INQUIRY SKILLS

There are mixed opinions within the science education community about teaching science process skills in isolation from each other and from the context of a scientific discipline. Rezba et al. (1995), who provide a series of lessons on individual process skills, warn that such an approach implies a separation of the process skills used in scientific work. They emphasize that these thinking skills are, in fact, interdependent and that in authentic scientific investigations the artificial separations will disappear.

Timing is an important consideration in introducing manipulative skills related to science processes and science equipment. Although safety procedures should be demonstrated and practiced early in the school year and repeated at intervals, other skills should be introduced as they are needed. For example, you might introduce data gathering methods using artificial data for practice purposes just before students are given an assignment requiring that they gather, display, and interpret data from a class experiment. Likewise, postpone teaching how to use a balance until you are ready to involve students in a meaningful learning activity requiring the measurement of mass. Avoid teaching isolated process skills and use of equipment only during the first week of school, when you know that the applications for them will be coming much later in the school year.

TEACHING ABOUT THE HISTORY AND NATURE OF SCIENCE

Instructional strategies based on biographies of scientists and research reports in popular and scientific publications enrich the science content study in each discipline. For example, when biology students confront the theory of evolution, use biographies as well as excerpts from Darwin's writings and from those of his contemporaries. Have students identify passages that confirm or refute ideas, such as these, to which they have been introduced: the tentativeness of scientific knowledge; the nature and role of theories; and the role of the scientific community in determining the acceptability of new scientific knowledge.

TEACHING REAL-WORLD APPLICATIONS

Many scientific principles addressed at the elementary and middle grades levels can be easily applied to students' lives. In planning instruction, those applications should be incorporated into teaching units as often as possible.

In higher level courses in high school, areas of sophisticated technical knowledge may have realistic applications only in industrial or medical fields. Although the applications to students' lives are not immediately obvious, they have an impact on our health and economic systems, influencing students indirectly. Invite scientists and engineers who use the theoretical knowledge in industrial or medical settings to your classroom. For example, have a textiles engineer explain to chemistry students how she uses the theoretical model of polymers to invent fibers with predictable properties. Ask a forensic scientist from your state crime lab to discuss applications of DNA science to his work. Resourceful teachers can almost always make connections that provoke student curiosity and interest.

REFERENCES

Ahlgren, A. (1996). How standards fit within the framework of science education reform. In J. Rhoton & P. Bowers (Eds.), *Issues in science education* (pp. 40–45). Washington, DC: National Science Teachers Association.

American Association for the Advancement of Science. (1993). *Benchmarks for science literacy.* New York: Oxford University Press.

American Association for the Advancement of Science. (1990). *Science for all Americans.* New York: Oxford University Press.

Arons, A.B. (1988). Historical and philosophical perspectives attainable in introductory physics courses. *Educational Philosophy and Theory, 20,* 13–23.

Bentley, M.L., & Garrison, J.W. (1991). The role of philosophy of science in science teacher education. *Journal of Science Teacher Education, 2,* 67–71.

Brown, J.H., & Shavelson, R.J. (1996). *Assessing hands-on science.* Thousand Oaks, CA: Corwin.

Bybee, R.W., & DeBoer, G.E. (1994). Research on goals for the science curriculum. In D.L. Gabel (Ed.), *Handbook of research on science teaching and learning* (pp. 357–387). New York: Macmillan.

Carter, G., & Berenson, S.B. (1996). Authentic assessment: Vehicle for reform. In J. Rhoton & P. Bowers (Eds.), *Issues in science education* (pp. 96–106). Washington, DC: National Science Teachers Association.

Cole, J. (1986). *The magic school bus at the waterworks.* New York: Scholastic.

Duschl, R.A. (1994). Research on the history and philosophy of science. In D.L. Gabel (Ed.), *Handbook of research on science teaching and learning* (pp. 443–465). New York: Macmillan.

Good, R., Herron, J., Lawson, A., & Renner, J. (1985). The domain of science education. *Science Education, 69,* 139–141.

Hofstein, A., & Yager, R. (1982). Societal issues as organizers for science education in the 80s. *School Science and Mathematics, 82,* 539–547.

Kendall, J.S., & Marzano, R.J. (1996). *Content knowledge.* Aurora, CO: Mid-continent Regional Educational Laboratory.

Lederman, N.G. (1992). Students' and teachers' conceptions of the nature of science: A review of the research. *Journal of Research in Science teaching, 29,* 331–359.

National Research Council. (1996). *National science education standards.* Washington, DC: National Academy Press.

National Science Teachers Association. (1992). *The content core.* Washington, DC: Author.

Rezba, R.J., Sprague, C.S., Fiel, R.L., Funk, H.J., Okey, J.R., & Jaus, H.H. (1995). *Learning and assessing science process skills* (3rd ed.). Dubuque, IA: Kendall/Hunt.

Tamir, P. (1985). Practical examinations. In T. Husen & N. Postlewaite (Eds.). *International encyclopedia of educational research.* London: Pergamon.

Wandersee, J.H. (1985). Can the history of science help science educators anticipate students' misconceptions? *Journal of Research in Science Teaching, 23,* 581–597.

8

USING THE ACHIEVEMENT CYCLE IN MATHEMATICS

John Parker

The *Curriculum and Evaluation Standards for School Mathematics* (1989) and its companion documents, the *Professional Standards for Teaching Mathematics* (1991) and the *Assessment Standards for School Mathematics* (1995) (three publications by the National Council of Teachers of Mathematics), have become the most widely referenced standards volumes in core academic disciplines. Unlike recent standards publications in other disciplines, these documents are not widely challenged as an appropriate blueprint for reform in mathematics education. When these books were published, mathematics educators foresaw the 1980s as a decade of research and the 1990s as a decade of implementation. However, as the end of "the decade of implementation" nears, there is evidence that the curriculum and instructional changes proposed are not experiencing significant, widespread use.

This chapter examines how the achievement cycle applies in mathematics.

USING THE MATHEMATICS STANDARDS TO DEVELOP CURRICULA

Mathematical power is a basic concept of the *Curriculum and Evaluation Standards*. Mathematical power is defined as "an individual's ability to explore, conjecture, and reason logically, as well as the ability to use a variety of mathematical methods effectively to solve nonroutine problems" (p. 5). Authors have written texts and resource materials focusing on problem solving and mathematical modeling in the last decade to enable schools to produce students with mathematical power. Problem-solving curricula typically begin by leading students through application of some general problem-solving strategies such as working backwards, making a table to organize given information, and guess and check. The mathematics content is then addressed by applying these strategies. *Algebra: A Process Approach* by Rachlin, Matsumoto, and Wada (1992) is one example of a textbook that uses this model.

Mathematical modeling has grown in popularity as technological tools have allowed students access to statistical methods and graphical interpretations of data that were previously unavailable except through tedious paper and pencil calculations. Mathematical modeling involves giving students a problem situation that lends itself to quantification or geometrical interpretation. Students are required to use their knowledge of mathematics to translate the problem parameters into a mathematical model, do mathematics within the context of the model to reach a mathematical answer, and interpret it in the original problem to determine a solution. The Consortium for Mathematics Applications (COMAP) publishes a series of materials that provide numerous modeling examples. Texts that use this applications-directed approach include *University of Chicago School Mathematics Project Series* (1992) and *Contemporary Precalculus Through Applications*, written by the mathematics department of the North Carolina School of Science and Mathematics (1989).

The *Standards* are organized into three grade spans, K-4, 5–8 and 9–12. There are 13 standards in the K-4 and 5–8 grade spans and 14 standards in the 9–12 grade span. Each grade span has four sets of standards that are not content-specific: mathematics as problem solving; mathematics as communication; mathematics as reasoning; and mathematical connections. Specific content standards complete the standards in each grade span. The content standards may be organized into four general areas: numeration and computation; geometry and measurement; patterns and relationships; and data analysis. Figure 8.1 summarizes the development of the general strands and Figure 8.2 (pp. 128–129), the development of the content strands among the three grade spans.

FIGURE 8.1. STANDARDS: GENERAL STRANDS

Grades K-4	Grades 5–8	Grades 9–12
Mathematics as problem solving	Mathematics as problem solving	Mathematics as problem solving
Use problem solving strategies as processes at all times to provide a context for skills and concepts to be learned.	Complete open-ended, extended projects that give students the opportunity to investigate and formulate new questions.	Form a basis for students doing and applying mathematics.
Mathematics as communication	Mathematics as communication	Mathematics as communication
Talk and write about mathematics as language skills are developed.	Explain, defend and conjecture mathematical ideas and develop a common language.	Personalize mathematics by clarifying, paraphrasing, and elaborating mathematical ideas.
Mathematics as reasoning	Mathematics as reasoning	Mathematics as reasoning
Develop mathematics as a logical, sensible and enjoyable pursuit.	Construct and evaluate arguments to defend ideas and formulate new ideas.	Formalize arguments by using deductive and inductive logic to defend arguments and propose new ideas in all areas of the curriculum.
Mathematical connections	Mathematical connections	Mathematical connections
Connect different representations of ideas and procedures to one another; use mathematics in other subjects and in life outside of school.	Regard mathematics as a unified subject; use various mathematical forms—graphical, numerical, algebraic and verbal—to represent problem solutions; identify the importance of mathematics in society.	Use the connections among branches of mathematics to apply its use in other disciplines and in the world outside of school.

FIGURE 8.2. STANDARDS: CONTENT STRANDS

Grades K-4	Grades 5–8	Grades 9–12
Numeration and computation Develop number sense by using estimation strategies, applying numeration systems, concepts of whole number operations, whole number computation skills and basic concepts of fractions.	Numeration and computation Improve number sense by using more sophisticated estimation techniques, exploring number relationships and number theory, computing with fractions and decimals and choosing appropriate operations and tools in problem situations.	Numeration and computation Develop the relationship between the system of real numbers and its various sub-systems; use these relationships to model real-world situations with number representations.
Geometry and measurement Develop spatial sense by manipulating shapes and working with the language of shapes; understand attributes of length, capacity, weight, area, volume, time, temperature, through informal investigations and beginning development of formal measurement systems.	Geometry and measurement Use geometric models by exploring transformations of geometric figures, applying geometric properties and relationships, using appropriate units and tools within measurement systems to get appropriate levels of accuracy, and developing concepts of rate and other derived, indirect and formulated measurements.	Geometry and measurement Develop the theory and relationships of two and three dimensional synthetic and coordinate geometric systems; use geometric models, concepts, and relationships, including congruence and similarity, vector analysis, and trigonometry to model real-world relationships.

Grades K-4	Grades 5–8	Grades 9–12
Patterns and relationships Explore a variety of patterns; represent and describe basic mathematical relationships.	Patterns and relationships Analyze relationships among changes in quantities, by using tables, graphs and rules; use basic algebraic principles such as linear equations and inequalities and coordinate geometry to solve problems.	Patterns and relationships Develop formal algebraic systems; explore maximum and minimum points of functions and investigate limits through sequences and series; use a variety of function representations to model real-world situations.
Data analysis Explore concepts of chance and data by collecting, organizing, describing, constructing, reading, and interpreting data displays.	Data analysis Use systematic collection of data to make inferences and construct logical arguments; devise and carry out simple probability experiments to deepen understanding of chance and begin development of probability formulas.	Data analysis Make predictions from data based on formal statistical methods; design experiments that rely on statistical procedures; connect experimental and theoretical probability techniques; use finite graphs, matrices, sequences, and recurrence relations as problem-solving tools.

STATUS OF THE STANDARDS

As implementation of the *Standards* is examined and feedback is received from teachers around the country, it has become apparent there is a need to update the *Standards*. As of this writing, the National Council of Teachers of Mathematics has approved plans to revise the three *Standards* documents into a single volume. The organization foresees reaffirming the philosophy of the earlier *Standards* publications, while posing new challenges for the future. The condensing of the three documents into one will support the "interrelationships among curriculum, teaching, and assessment" (National Council of Teachers of Mathematics, 1997, p. 1). A draft will be released in fall 1998 with the final version available in 2000.

Unlike the modern math reform movement of the 1960s, the standards reform movement was conceptualized as a long-term process. It has been more carefully planned with a broader cross-section of input and endorsements. As a result, the *Standards 2000* revision will be an enhancement of the previous publications rather than a reactionary movement like the "back to basics" trend of the 1970s.

The *Curriculum and Evaluation Standards* were written by teams of mathematics educators representing elementary, secondary and college levels. Support was garnered from a variety of professional organizations including the American Federation of Teachers, the National Society for Professional Engineers, and the National Congress of Parents and Teachers. Public relations briefs stressing the need for reform in mathematics education, were written and widely publicized prior to release of the *Standards*. Planning implementation over a long period of time and securing involvement of various constituencies have made it more likely that the standards reform movement in mathematics will be of lasting consequence.

Lynne Cheney (1997) in her *New York Times* column equates the mathematics standards movement to the "modern math" reform era of the 1960s. Cheney attacks the *Standards*, borrowing from the emotional national debate on reading instruction by calling the *Standards* movement "whole" mathematics. Criticisms like this have appeared during the past eight years. The criticisms complain chiefly about the reduced emphasis on computation skills and basic knowledge of algebra.

Thomas Romberg (1997) effectively counters this criticism in the same issue by stating that the *Standards* do not propose eliminating mastery of basic operational facts. He reemphasizes that current computational mathematics instruction should be based on balancing mental math, estimation, calculator use, and paper and pencil arithmetic. He acknowledges that students need to know basic skills, but states, "they need to be able to deduce and induce from context and formulate counter examples. They need to be able to apply spatial, proportional, algebraic and graphic reasoning, and to construct proofs" (p. A13).

Among professional educators, the philosophy of the *Standards* as embodied in the concept of mathematical power is practically unquestioned. However, there have been technical criticisms of their organization and vocabulary. The most significant criticism is the alleged disconnection between developmental levels. For example, as Kendall and Marzano (1996) note, knowledge and skills categorized in grade-span 5–8 may not have a developmental relationship to the same knowledge and skills strand in grade-span K-4. Some education specialists disagree with the use of the word "standards," suggesting that NCTM's standards are not specific enough to be true measurable standards. These criticisms have not impeded the progress of state curriculum work that uses the *Standards* as a guide. Most states revised their mathematics curricula to reflect recommendations from the *Standards* within five years of the release of the original edition. Several states are writing curriculum frameworks that are less prescriptive than their original revisions.

One purpose of these frameworks is to accommodate recommendations from state study groups to allow more teacher flexibility and to be more conducive to designing broader accountability assessments. In North Carolina, state tests designed to measure students' knowledge and application of the content of the state curriculum in Grades 3 through 8 have been used since 1993. Performance on the multiple choice portions of these tests has improved gradually since their inception. As part of the 1993 tests, all students answered open-ended questions that required writing explanations about their reasoning. These questions were evaluated by teachers who underwent intensive training to ensure evaluator reliability. The cost of scoring these questions and the lack of understanding of the published results precluded continued use of these questions. In 1997, students in Grades 5 and 8 were given similar open-ended questions, graded by evaluators from an outside agency. The performance on these open-ended questions was significantly lower than performance on the multiple choice questions. This is another indication that problem solving, reasoning, communication, and connections are not regular requirements in mathematics classrooms.

Recognition of needed standards-based reform and curricular adjustments on the state level have not produced significant change in American classrooms. The Third International Mathematics and Science Study (U.S. Department of Education, 1997) gives evidence that traditional behaviorist approaches to organizing mathematics instruction as distinct packets of information still dominate American K-12 education. This study includes assessments of student achievement, surveys of students and teachers, analyses of curriculum materials, videotapes of classes in Germany, Japan, and the United States, and case studies of teaching contexts. This study supports the direction outlined in the *Standards*, but indicates that classes in other countries come closer to using *Standards* based practices.

Findings from this report state that eighth-grade lessons in the United States, "emphasize acquisition of skills in lessons that follow this pattern:

1. Teacher instructs students in a concept or skill.

2. Teacher solves example problems with class.

3. Students practice on their own while the teacher assists individual students" (p. 42).

The nations involved in the same study, whose students typically outperform American students on international comparisons, use lessons that begin with a problem, have students presenting various possible solutions, and conclude with the teacher summarizing the class findings.

SUMMARY: CURRICULUM STANDARDS IN MATHEMATICS

Figure 8.3, on pages 134–135 , summarizes the status of standards in mathematics and recommends how they might best be used by school systems.

PERFORMANCE ASSESSMENT IN MATHEMATICS

Webb and Briars (1990) describe assessment as "an interaction between teacher and students, with the teacher continually seeking to understand what a student can do and how a student is able to do it and then using this information to guide instruction" (1990, p. 108). The emphasis being placed on high-stakes accountability evaluation measures in conjunction with a history of viewing mathematics through a behaviorist lens has moved mathematics classroom assessment far from this ideal.

The evaluation section of the *Curriculum and Evaluation Standards* lists six areas for "decreased attention" that have characterized assessment in traditional mathematics classrooms. These are:

- assessing what students do not know;
- counting correct answers on tests for the sole purpose of assigning grades;
- focusing on a large number of specific and isolated skills organized by a content-behavior matrix;
- using exercises or word problems requiring only one or two skills;
- using only written tests;
- excluding calculators, computers, and manipulatives from the assessment process. (p. 191)

FIGURE 8.3. SUMMARY: CURRICULUM
STANDARDS IN MATHEMATICS

Primary sources

> Kendall, J.S., & Marzano, R.J. (1996). *Continent knowledge.* Aurora, CO: Mid-continent Regional Educational Laboratory.
>
> National Council of Teachers of Mathematics. (1995). *Assessment standards for school mathematics.* Reston, VA: Author.
>
> National Council of Teachers of Mathematics. (1989). *Curriculum and evaluation standards for school mathematics.* Reston, VA: Author.
>
> National Council of Teachers of Mathematicsw. (1991). *Professional standards for teaching mathematics.* Reston, VA: Author.

Strands used

> The NCTM report has 13 or 14 strands, depending upon the grade level. Problem solving, communication, reasoning and connections are used in all grade spans. Grades K-4 strands include: estimation; number sense and numeration; concepts of whole number operations; whole number computation; geometry and spatial sense; measurement; statistics and probability; fractions and decimals; and patterns and relationships.
>
> Grades 5–8 content strands include: number and number relationships; number systems and number theory; computation and estimation; patterns and functions; algebra; statistics; probability; geometry; and measurement.
>
> Grades 9–12 strands include the following: algebra; functions; geometry from a synthetic perspective; geometry from an algebraic perspective; trigonometry; statistics; probability; discrete mathematics; conceptual underpinnings of calculus; and mathematical structure.
>
> The Kendall/Marzano compilation organizes standards in nine strands: problem solving; numeratiion; computation; measurement; geometry; data analysis and distributions; probability and statistics; functions and algebra; and nature and uses of mathematics.

Subject organization

No subject organization is identified in any of the reports cited. High schools often use a subject organization based on ability levels, similar to the following:

Noncollege bound: prealgebra; Algebra 1; math applications.

College preparatory: Algebra 1; geometry; Algebra 2; advanced algebra and trigonometry.

Honors: Algebra 1; Algebra 2; advanced algebra and trigonometry; calculus.

The NCTM standards recommend a core body of knowledge for all students with advanced courses designed to enrich this core knowledge. Some high schools have begun using a "unified math" approach that integrates algebra, geometry, and advanced topics.

Summary of standards

The NCTM standards are organized into three grade spans: K-4; 5–8; 9–12. Kendall and Marzano use four grade spans: K-2; 3–5; 6–8; 9–12. The NCTM standards use four strands that are not content-specific: mathematics as problem solving; mathematics as communication; mathematics as reasoning; mathematical connections. Content standards may be organized into four general areas: numeration and computation; geometry and measurement; patterns and relationships; data analysis.

Recommendations to school districts

♦ Correlate state content standards with the Kendall/Marzano analysis.

♦ Determine subject organization.

♦ Analyze and correlate standards that are not content-specific (such as problem solving, communication, reasoning, and connections), using state, Kendall/Marzano, and NCTM reports.

♦ Identify grade level benchmarks from this analysis.

These assessment characteristics are closely related to the types of exercises and problems students are assigned. Mathematics has often been considered a discipline in which student achievement can be easily and reliably assessed. This perception exists because most mathematics teachers have evaluated students by considering answers "right" or "wrong." Consider this example of a problem: $1/4 + 2/3 = ?$. If a student answers "3/7," a typical reaction is to mark the answer wrong and assume the student incorrectly applies the addition algorithm for fractions by adding the numerators and denominators of the fractions. The teacher who merely corrects the answer on the basis of "typical" mistakes has devalued the student's number sense, which can be used to improve his operation sense.

If the exercise requests an explanation of how the student arrives at the answer, the teacher will get valuable diagnostic information and the opportunity to reward the student for what he knows. Consider the difference between asking the student to "give the sum of $1/4$ and $2/3$" and asking the student to "give the sum of $1/4$ and $2/3$ and explain how you get the sum using pictures, manipulatives, or examples as needed."

For the first exercise, some teachers will evaluate the result as right or wrong only. More diligent teachers will require the student to show his work and develop an evaluation guide for rewarding parts of the fraction addition algorithm the student completes. Consider the addition process in this example.

$$\text{Common denominator} = 12$$
$$
\begin{array}{r}
1/4 = \ \ 3/12 \\
+ \ \ 2/3 = \ \ 8/12 \\
\hline
11/12 = \text{sum}
\end{array}
$$

If the teacher decides that this example is worth three points, the teacher might award one point for correctly identifying a common denominator, one point for converting $1/4$ and $2/3$ to equivalent fractions with a denominator of 12, and one point for correctly completing the addition.

For the adapted version of the exercise ("give the sum of $1/4$ and $2/3$ and explain how you get the sum using pictures, manipulatives, or examples as needed"), the teacher must set up an evaluation plan that includes the quality of the student's explanation. This version allows the teacher to get more information from students who have not yet mastered the related algorithm, but who may be developing legitimate ideas. The teacher will have a common language to share with the students as they build on their understanding of fraction concepts. Referencing the *Standards* curriculum strands (Figures 8.1 (p. 127) and 8.2 (pp. 128–129)), the teacher might ask these questions to plan an evaluation guide:

- Is the student's response logical? (mathematics as reasoning)

- Does the student use appropriate fraction concepts? (K-4 numeration and computation)

- Does the student clearly convey his or her thoughts and the solution? (mathematics as communication)

From these guiding questions, the teacher might write the three-point evaluation rubric shown in Figure 8.4, on the next page.

Asking for an explanation of the student's method for solving the problem and evaluating the explanation by linking to standards serve several useful purposes. Doing so broadens the teacher's capacity to determine what the student knows, allowing the student more ways to show what the student knows. If the teacher uses evaluation processes such as this consistently, students realize the teacher values more than a correct answer derived from a set procedure. Over time, this evaluation process helps students understand that mathematics has a unifying logic, rather than being a set of disconnected rules and procedures.

An important feature of performance-based assessment theory is sharing the evaluation guide with the students as the problem is assigned. The rubric in Figure 8.4 is written in the author's language. To share with the students, it must be translated into language appropriate for their developmental level. Figure 8.5 (p. 139) illustrates an attempt to write the rubric on a 4th grade level.

FIGURE 8.4. EVALUATION RUBRIC FOR FRACTION ADDITION

	Logic	Fraction Concepts	Communication
2	Student follows a logical sequence of steps to an accurate conclusion.	Student understands basic fraction concepts, equivalent fractions and the concept of fraction addition.	Student communicates reasoning and solution clearly and concisely, using appropriate words, illustrations, manipulatives, or other prompts as needed.
1	Student follows a logical sequence of steps but there is some misunderstanding that prevents the student from reaching an accurate conclusion.	Student understands basic fraction concepts but is confused about some of the connections between the basic concepts and equivalent fractions and/or fraction addition.	Student communicates reasoning and response using words, illustrations, manipulatives, or other prompts; however, communication could be clearer by adding more information or omitting extraneous information.
0	Student response is illogical.	Student does not understand basic fraction concepts.	Student makes no effort to communicate reasoning or results.

FIGURE 8.5. STUDENT RUBRIC FOR FRACTION ADDITION

	Logic	Fraction Concepts	Communication
Solution to the problem is complete, accurate and well-communicated.	Each step in your problem solving sequence leads logically to the next step	You demonstrate an understanding of the meaning of fractions, equivalent fractions and fraction addition.	You communicated your logic and conclusion clearly without leaving out any essential information or giving any extra information. Your use of examples, manipulatives or diagrams made your explanation better.
Continue working on the problem to improve the areas noted.	Most of your steps are logically connected, but some are not.	You understand basic fraction concepts, but need to think about how these concepts relate to equivalent fractions and fraction addition.	You communicated your logic and solution in a way that I could understand, but you left out some important information or included some extra information. Your use of examples, manipulatives or diagrams helped me understand your explanation.

	Logic	Fraction Concepts	Communication
Another problem like this will be assigned to give you another chance. I will work with you to improve.	You need to put more thought into this problem.	We need to review basic fraction concepts.	You need to explain your solution and the logic that led to your solution.

Comparison of the traditional problem and the revised problem illustrates how a problem and the teacher's evaluation may be adapted to direct students toward more thoughtful habits of mind in mathematics classes. The traditional problem has only one solution route with a few possible variations. A teacher might develop these questions to evaluate students' answers to this problem on a test.

- Is the translation to a numerical expression correct?

- Is the arithmetic done correctly?

- Is the solution correct and is it communicated correctly?

A scheme might be devised to assign points for each question with the teacher weighting each question based on its relative importance. Assume for whatever reasons the teacher is awarding six points for doing all three steps correctly. Some possible evaluation schemes are illustrated in Figure 8.6.

FIGURE 8.6. TRADITIONAL PROBLEM EVALUATION SCHEMES

Translation	Arithmetic	Communication of solution	Description of evaluation scheme
2 points	2 points	2 points	Each is weighted equally.
3 points	2 points	1 point	More emphasis is put on translation; little emphasis on communicating the solution.

Note how each of the evaluation questions relates to the student doing something correctly within a narrow range of possibilities. This is due to the nature of the problem, which is directed toward a specific way of thinking.

Compare this evaluation method to one that uses performance-based assessment to evaluate the student. The teacher might develop these questions that relate directly to the K-4 *Standards* strands in Figures 8.1 (p. 127) and 8.2 (pp. 128–129).

- ◆ (Mathematics as problem solving, mathematics as reasoning, and mathematical connections) Does the student show evidence of logical reasoning and application of appropriate problem solving strategies? Such evidence might be given by the student's beginning exploration of the problem using specific arithmetic operations to compute the costs of possible combinations of items and comparison of their total to 50 cents. Further evidence might be organizing random trials into some logical pattern of thought and constructing a logical argument in communicating the results of her work.

- ◆ (K-4 numeration and computation, concepts of whole number operations, and whole number computation skills) Does the student apply appropriate arithmetic operations and are the arithmetic operations performed accurately?

- ◆ (Mathematics as communication) Does the student write clearly about what the student is doing and what the student knows?

Applying the same three-point scheme, a rubric can be constructed that blends the elements of the three questions. Each evaluation question is given equal weight. Linking the problem to standards and designing the problem so there are different ways to proceed allows for a more open evaluation scheme. Figure 8.7, on the next page, illustrates a rubric for the revised problem.

Writing rubrics as evaluation guides is a time consuming, thoughtful process. There are numerous resources available with generic rubrics that can be adapted to fit the needs of the

FIGURE 8.7. RUBRIC FOR REVISED PROBLEM

	Reasoning, application of problem solving strategies and mathematical connections	Concepts of whole numbers and whole number computation skills	Communication
2	The problem is translated into one or more appropriate mathematical expressions; these expressions are organized and connected in a logical fashion that leads to a logical conclusion.	Appropriate arithmetic operations are applied; all computations are accurate.	The solution and the logic leading to the solution are communicated clearly and concisely.
1	The problem is translated into at least one appropriate mathematical expression; there is evidence that the student is trying to logically connect the translation(s) to a method for solving the problem.	Appropriate arithmetic operations are applied; there are some computation inaccuracies.	The solution and the logic leading to the solution are communicated in an understandable fashion. There is information omitted or information given that could be omitted that detracts from the clarity of the explanation.
0	There is no evidence of connecting the essential elements of the problem to numerical or alternative representations.	Inappropriate arithmetic operations are applied; computations that are shown are inaccurate.	There is no attempt to communicate the student's work.

teacher. The rubric for the preceding example was written after reviewing the literature (Wessels & Birkholtz, 1991; Petit & Zuwojewski, 1997; Marzano, Pickering, & McTighe, 1993.) The process began by first establishing the low achievement level and the high achievement level and filling in the intermediate portion of the scale. Assessment experts recommend that teachers should assess the students and adjust the rubric for future use after analyzing how the students approach the problem and solve it. Presenting the rubric at the same time the problem is presented gives a consistent basis for improving the student product and discussing how the student is thinking as the student progresses. However, the first version of the rubric should be revised after gaining valuable information through dialogue with the students. Revisions will make it more usable for future assessments. Sample rubrics for each level of performance can be used to show models to future classes.

USING ASSESSMENT-DRIVEN INSTRUCTION IN MATH

Figure 8.8 gives a framework for comparing traditional mathematics curriculum and instruction and the *Standards'* recommendations for change. It is adapted from *The Curriculum and Evaluation Standards for School Mathematics* (p. 146).

FIGURE 8.8. A FRAMEWORK FOR COMPARISON

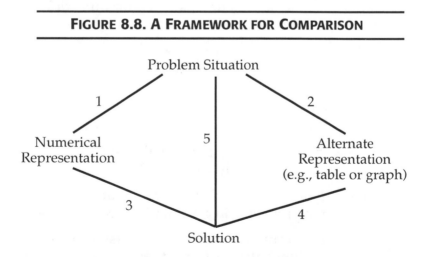

Traditional mathematics curricula have addressed the left side of the cycle represented in the diagram in discrete parts. Now, computer graphing tools and graphing calculators give teachers access to alternative representations of problems (Figure 8.8, line 2). In traditional textbooks, several chapters or sets of exercises within chapters emphasize translating a contrived problem situation to a numerical or algebraic representation. The major part of traditional curricula focuses on algebraic and numerical processing (Figure 8.8, line 3). A discussion of a traditional elementary problem compared to an adapted version of the same problem follows. Figure 8.8 is used as a context for discussion of the problems.

TRADITIONAL PROBLEM

> Mary Jo has $1.00 to buy supplies from the student store. One pencil costs 10 cents, one eraser costs 5 cents and one pack of paper costs 40 cents. Mary Jo buys two pencils, two erasers and one pack of paper. How much does she spend? How much money does she get back?

Solving this problem involves recognizing the relationship between the unit costs of the objects and the number purchased; applying the appropriate operations of multiplication, addition, and subtraction; and communicating the answers. Referencing Figure 8.8, these steps might describe a solution process:

- Step 1 (Figure 8.8, line 1): Translate to a numerical representation.

  Total cost = 2x10 + 2x5 + 1x40

- Step 2 (Figure 8.8, line 3): Numerical processes.

  2x10 + 2x5 + 1x40 = 70; mathematical solution = 70

  $1 = 100 cents; 100 − 70 = 30

- Step 3 (Figure 8.8, line 5): Translate solution back to original problem and communicate results.

Mary Jo spends 70 cents. She receives 30 cents in change.

This example illustrates the type of "story problem" used in traditional texts as part of culminating sets of problems designed to have the student apply skills in a straight forward progression. Most teachers get students to solve these problems by spending a great deal of time drilling students on numerical processing (represented by line 3 in Figure 8.8), followed by examples like the one given that require students to use their basic skills in a routine setting. The repeated use of certain problem types encourages teachers to direct students to memorize translation procedures. These instructional patterns reduce learning mathematics to rote replication of rules.

An evaluation of this instructional pattern using the four general *Standards* strands indicates that traditional mathematics instruction only addresses these skills on a superficial level. In addition, the breadth of content suggested in the specific content strands cannot be reached. Consider how the same examples might be adapted to better relate to the *Standards* notions of problem solving, communication, reasoning and connections in mathematics, while addressing more of the content standards and increasing the potential for use of alternate representations of problem situations as represented by line 2 in Figure 8.8.

AUTHENTIC ASSESSMENT VERSION OF PROBLEM

> Mary Jo has 50 cents to spend at the student store. One pencil costs 10 cents, one eraser costs 5 cents, and one pack of paper costs 40 cents. Give as many ways as you can that Mary Jo can spend her money on these items and receive change. Have you identified all possible ways? Explain how you know you have stated all possible ways or how you know there are more ways.

This problem involves the same requisite knowledge as the traditional version, but encourages the student to explore a variety of possibilities using the arithmetic operations with different combinations of numbers. Drill with the arithmetic operations is built into a problem solving investigation. As students explore the different options, they are encouraged to organize their work in a table or an organized list, an important problem solving strategy.

Although solution approaches may vary, one possibility presented in the context of Figure 8.8 is:

- Step 1 (Figure 8.8, line 1): Translate to a numerical representation.

  Total cost = number of pencils x 10 + number of erasers x 5 + number of packs off paper x 40

  Students may start by considering a specific number of each item.

- Step 2 (Figure 8.8, line 3): Numerical processes.

  1x10 + 1x5 + 1x40 = 55 > 50 (no)

  2x10 + 0x5 + 1x40 = 60 > 50 (no)

  1x10 + 1x5 + 0x40 = 15 < 50 (yes)

  2x10 + 1x5 + 0x40 = 25 < 50 (yes)

  1x10 + 2x5 + 0x40 = 20 < 50 (yes)

  2x10 + 2x5 + 0x40 = 30 < 50 (yes)

- Step 3 (Figure 8.8, line 2): Organize arithmetic combinations into a table.

  After experimenting the student recognizes that Mary Jo can buy no more than one pack of paper. The student also knows that with one pack of paper there are only two possible options: zero erasers and zero pencils or one eraser and zero pencils. The student develops the strategy of keeping two items constant and varying the others, deciding to use a table similar to Figure 8.9 to organize this information.

  Using the table, the student reasons that three pencils are worth 30 cents, so the student can begin with no more than three erasers; thus, there will be four possible ways with three pencils, two possible ways with four pencils, and none with five pencils. Adding the two possibilities with one pack of paper, the student claims there are 31 (9 + 8 + 6 + 4 + 2 + 2 = 31) possible ways to purchase materials with 50 cents and receive change.

FIGURE 8.9. PROBLEM-SOLVING TABLE

Erasers	Pencils	Paper	Total	Change	Does it work?
10x5	0x10	0x40	50	0	no
9x5	0x10	0x40	45	5	yes
etc. 9 possible ways 1–9 erasers	etc.	etc.	etc.	etc.	etc.
9x5	1x10	0x40	55	0	no
8x5	1x10	0x40	50	0	no
7x5	1x10	0x40	45	5	yes
etc. 8 possible ways 0–7 erasers	etc.	etc.	etc.	etc.	etc.
7x5	2x10	0x40	55	0	no
6x5	2x10	0x40	50	0	no
5x5	2x10	0x40	45	5	yes
4x5	2x10	0x40	40	10	yes
etc. 6 possible ways 0–5 erasers	Etc.	etc.	etc.	etc.	etc.

- Step 4 (Figure 8.8, line 5): Translate solution back to original problem and communicate results. The student uses the table and explains his or her reasoning to communicate the results. Admittedly, few students will develop "clean" solutions like this. However, the teacher can set standards for evaluating the student's work based on expectations for student performance. The problem gives possibilities for students to drill on arithmetic skills while thinking about emerging patterns. Communicating their thinking requires additional in-depth thinking and supports their language development and writing proficiency.

Developing authentic assessment examples from traditional examples requires thinking about how the same mathematics content knowledge can be more closely associated with "real world" applications and how the requirements of the problem can be broadened to consolidate higher levels of reasoning and more avenues of communication. Typically, by making an association with "real-world" applications, higher levels of reasoning and more varied communication possibilities will develop, because "real-world" examples rarely fit a mathematical formulation. The previous example can be revised so the student has to think of different ways to spend Mary Jo's money. Exploring different ways to spend money is something adults do on a regular basis. The requirement of translating a more natural problem to a mathematical representation and interpreting the mathematical solution back in the original problem entails a higher level of reasoning. In addition, communicating the results means having better proficiency with written or spoken language skills.

Many teachers are reluctant to abandon traditional problems and instruction patterns, while incorporating nonroutine problems that require different instructional approaches. There are two major areas that need to be addressed to help facilitate this change.

First, assessing what is quality work on more complex problems requires thinking by the teacher that goes beyond right and wrong answers or simple assignment of points for showing an appropriate procedure. Performance assessment theory gives a structure for setting standards for students and evaluating their work.

Second, traditional problems are not totally abandoned; rather, they are used to prepare students to solve more complex problems. The number of traditional problems must be reduced to allow time for students to put quality thought into solving complex problems. Any change in time allocation requires thoughtful planning. The assessment cycle serves as a planning tool for making this change.

DESIGNING ASSESSMENT-BASED UNITS IN MATHEMATICS

An assessment-based unit begins by selecting a performance task that meets the criteria identified in Chapter 3 and is connected to the curriculum standards. Imagine a middle grades teacher whose year plan calls for him to teach a beginning unit on data analysis. His primary goal is to have students use systematic collection of data to make inferences and construct logical arguments (see Figure 8.2, pages 128–129, middle grades "Data Analysis" strand). He recognizes that his students need to review fraction arithmetic and need to improve their understanding of percentages (see Figure 8.2, middle grades "Numeration and Computation" strand). In addition, he wants to incorporate requirements that give his students opportunities to reason, communicate mathematical ideas and connect mathematics to meaningful applications (see Figure 8.1, page 127, "Standards: General Strands"). Part of his professional development plan for the year is to increase the use of calculators and computers as instructional tools in his classes.

To accomplish these goals, he designs this task for his students.

> Belmont Middle School is working hard to win the Superintendent's Attendance Banner. To win this award students must average 95% attendance for the year. Mr. Cumbo's 6th-grade class has decided to analyze how the school is doing at the end of first semester so they can encourage students to

win the attendance prize. Ms. Moses, their principal, has given them the following data for August through December.

Month	Average total students enrolled each day	Number of school days	Average number of students present each day
August	545	14	530
September	547	24	524
October	550	21	520
November	549	16	519
December	549	14	518

Analyze these data to determine how Belmont is doing. Write a report on your findings. Include in your report:

(1) The school's current status and how that was determined;

(2) The necessary average monthly attendance for the second semester in order for Belmont to earn the Superintendent's Attendance Banner. Explain how you determined that.

Be prepared to discuss your findings with the principal, knowing she will have questions about how you projected the required attendance for second semester and will want suggestions for ensuring that the school's attendance meets the goal.

With the performance task written, the teacher now does a task analysis of the problem and defines performance expectations. These performance standards will be shared with the students at the beginning of the unit. The performance standards are linked directly to the curriculum standards upon which the unit focuses. Doing a task analysis and defining performance standards at the outset of planning give the teacher a framework for writing the entire unit. As the teacher is doing these steps, he may realize the need to make adjustments in the problem.

The following is a sample task analysis of this problem:

- Make reasonable estimates of 95% of various numbers leading to a reasonable estimate of 95% of 550. "Number sense" questions leading to a reasonable estimate could be: "What is 95% of 100? 95% of 200?…95% of 500? 95% of 600? and 95% of 550?"

- Know that percentage of students present is computed by dividing number of students present by total number of students. Relate percentages to common fractions and operation of division.

- Use calculator to efficiently compute totals and percentages.

- Display monthly percentages to study attendance trend.

- Distinguish between the monthly average of percent present and the actual total percent present and know why these numbers are different.

- Write about and describe the process of calculating the first semester attendance.

- Present the monthly attendance percentages and describe the trend in a descriptive graph.

- Analyze possible reasons for the trend and project what may happen second semester.

- Discover what information might be helpful to analyze second semester trends.

- Write a concluding report and discuss findings with the teacher and the principal.

The teacher decides that he will define performance standards in four areas: mathematics as reasoning, mathematics as communication, data analysis, and numeration and computation. He devises the rubric shown in Figure 8.10 on the next page.

FIGURE 8.10. EVALUATION RUBRIC FOR ATTENDANCE PROBLEM

	Reasoning	Data Analysis	Numeration & Computation	Communication
Report is ready for the principal.	Data from first semester is used to make a projection to second semester. Data from previous years is requested and used to make recommendations.	Data is presented clearly in appropriate tables and graphs. First semester graphs help project attendance trend and graphs of previous years' attendance support recommendations.	Logical estimation strategies are employed. Computations are accurate. Efficient use of calculators and or computers is used to manage all the computations.	A clear description of the data and recommendations for second semester is given. Text and graphs and tables are presented neatly and effectively.
Some improvements need to be made in your report.	Data from first semester is projected to second semester. Data from previous years is used. Connections between the two sets of data are not made.	Data is organized and tabulated. Graphs are presented to project first semester attendance and graphs of previous years' attendance are given. Some of the information in the graphs is not clear.	Logical estimation strategies are used. There are some inaccurate computations and/or calculators or computers are not used in the most efficient manner.	The final report to Ms. Moses is completed. It is well prepared, but could be improved by clearer descriptions or graphical displays.

| You have the beginning of an adequate report. | Connections between the data and recommendations are made, but some conclusions and recommendations are illogical. | The data is organized with some computations tabulated. The data is not presented in a graph that can be used to understand the attendance trend. | There is evidence of a lack of understanding of percentages. There are computational inaccuracies and the computations are not organized to be done efficiently with calculators or computers. | The final report is started, but is incomplete. |

He is now ready to do a detailed plan of the unit that will lead to successful student performance. Figure 8.11 is a template of a guide used in one school district to help mathematics teachers design assessment-based units.

FIGURE 8.11. ASSESSMENT-BASED UNIT PLANNING TEMPLATE

Reasoning and problem solving skills and concepts:
Communication links:
Connections to other disciplines and "real-world" situations:

State content standards:

National content standards:

Statement of beginning problem or performance task:

Evaluation guide for student performance:

Teacher resources: Student resources:

Brief overview of unit:

A CONCLUDING NOTE

Making the transition from traditional mathematics assessment practices to those recommended in this chapter will require concerted time and effort. Professional development plans that attempt to quickly insert a "canned" method to generate authentic teaching practices will not work. Convincing teachers of the need to change is a first step in any professional development plan of this nature. That alone can take an extended period of time and will not happen to whole groups of teachers at once. This chapter is based primarily on ideas generated by teachers who were given extended release time from class and who were paid to write curriculum in the summer. They recognized at the outset the need to change, and know that translating their planning into practice is another major challenge. This chapter has provided a framework that educators can use as a filter for their own ideas in initiating long overdue changes in mathematics instruction and assessment.

REFERENCES

Cheney, L. (1997, August 11). Once again, basic skills fall prey to a fad. *New York Times*, p. A13.

Kendall, J.S., & Marzano, R.J. (1996). *Content knowledge.* Aurora, CO: Mid-continent Regional Educational Laboratory.

Marzano, R.J., Pickering, D., & McTighe J. (1993). *Assessing student outcomes.* Alexandria, VA: Association for Supervision and Curriculum Development.

National Council of Teachers of Mathematics. (1989). *Curriculum and evaluation standards for school mathematics.* Reston, VA: Author.

National Council of Teachers of Mathematics. (1991). *Professional standards for teaching mathematics.* Reston, VA: Author.

National Council of Teachers of Mathematics. (1995). *Assessment standards for school mathematics.* Reston, VA: Author.

National Council of Teachers of Mathematics. (1997, January 29). *The future of the NCTM standards: Our current status.* (On-line). Available: www.nctm.org. Author.

North Carolina School of Science and Mathematics. (1989). *Contemporary precalculus through applications.* Chicago: Everyday Learning.

Petit, M. & Sawojewski, J. S. (1997). Teachers and students learning together about assessing problem solving. *Mathematics Teacher, 90* (6), 472–477.

Rachlin, S.L., Matsumoto, A., & Wada, L.A. (1992). *Algebra: A process approach*. Honolulu: University of Hawaii Curriculum, Research, and Development Group.

Romberg, T. (1997, August 11). Mediocre is not enough. *New York Times*, p. A13.

University of Chicago School Mathematics Project Series. (1992). Glenview, IL: Scott Foresman.

U.S. Department of Education. (1997). Teaching. In *Pursuing excellence*. (On-line). Available: www.ed.gov. Author.

Webb, N., & Briars, D. (1990). Assessment in mathematics classrooms, K-8. In T. Cooney (Ed.), *Teaching and learning mathematics in the 1990s*. Reston, VA: National Council of Teachers of Mathematics.

Wessels, J.D., & Birkholz, C. (Eds.). (1991). *Rubrics and other tools for teaching quality*. North Mankato, MN: Ten Sigma.

9

THE ACHIEVEMENT CYCLE IN ENGLISH LANGUAGE ARTS

English language arts has received considerable attention with respect to standards and performance assessments, although only a few articles have dealt with assessment-driven instruction. Much of this attention to the development of standards has taken the form of contentious controversy. We caution you to proceed with due deliberation, securing teacher and community input throughout the process.

The following discussion suggests a process to use in developing standards, designing performance assessments, and using assessment-driven instruction.

DEVELOPING STANDARDS IN ENGLISH LANGUAGE ARTS

The process explained here will enable you to produce a set of useful and acceptable standards.

DECIDE ON THE STRANDS AND STANDARDS

The first step is to decide which strands to use in the development of standards. English language arts is usually conceptualized as including four general strands: reading; writing; listening; and speaking. Kendall and Marzano (1996) divide the subject in this manner: writing; reading; speaking and listening; literature; language. This author (Glatthorn, 1995) has used these strands successfully in several district curriculum projects:

Reading and literature: responses to literature; literary terms and concepts; required literary works.

Writing: several types emphasized at each grade
level.

Language study: language structure and concepts;
language history; language varieties, including
dialects.

Speaking and listening: special skills required for
more formal occasions.

Mass media and information processing: using
mass media; processing information.

The issue can be resolved by surveying teachers and discussing the results with them, because the only consideration is
teacher acceptance and understanding.

Once the strands have been identified, you can use them
to delineate the standards. The general standards can be derived by reviewing several sources, including these: Kendall
and Marzano, 1996; National Council of Teachers of Eng-
lish/International Reading Association, 1996; Speech Communication Association, 1996; Smagorinsky, 1996; and the
standards published by the your state's department of education. Because there seems to be general agreement on the
high-level standards, this task should not be difficult. Most
English language arts teachers would endorse this standard
for the writing strand (Kendall & Marzano, 1996):

Demonstrates competence in the general skills and
strategies of the writing process. (p. 294)

DECIDE ABOUT THE USE OF SPECIFIC BENCHMARKS

Once the strands have been determined, you should decide whether you want to add specific grade-level benchmarks, a matter of considerable controversy in the profession
and among interested citizens. The standards developed by
the National Council of Teachers of English (NCTE) and the
International Reading Association (IRA) (1996) include only
12 general statements of processes that students are to use.
Here is an example: "Students read a wide range of literature
from many periods in many genres to build an understanding of the many dimensions...of human experience" (p. 25).

Those general standards are supported with a more detailed explanation and rationale, but no benchmarks are provided. Supplementary materials published by NCTE continue to avoid such specifications, providing only "exemplars" showing how the standards might be operationalized in the best classrooms. (See Myers & Spalding, 1997.)

Maloney (1997) has criticized the NCTE/IRA standards for their vagueness, pointing out that they do not provide sufficient guidance at a time when students' achievements in and attitudes about English are questionable. On the other hand, Brewbaker (1997) argues that the lack of specifics derives from a view of the subject that emphasizes the holistic use of language, not one that sees it as a collection of fragmented skills.

The issue is one that needs careful study and deliberation, because it seems to elicit strong feelings in partisans on both sides of the issue. We recommend the use of a minimum number of benchmarks that are limited to the "mastery" objectives—those that require structured teaching and assessment. (See Glatthorn, 1994, for a fuller explication of the mastery curriculum theory.) Another compromise solution is to use only standards in grades K-4 and add benchmarks for the remaining levels. The discussion that follows assumes that you have decided to use benchmarks for the mastery objectives.

ANALYZE THE BENCHMARKS

To begin this task of developing district benchmarks, you should analyze the benchmarks specified in the publications noted above and any other current sources. Benchmarks in English can be of three types.

Mastery Benchmark

These benchmarks identify key concepts and skills that seem to require explicit teaching, that are likely to be tested, that are essential for all students, and that should be emphasized at one or two grade levels. The following is a Grades 6–8 benchmark from the Kendall/Marzano compilation that meets these criteria:

> Understands the concept of a "likely informant"
> for obtaining information about a specific topic.
> (p. 305)

As a mastery benchmark, that concept might be taught at Grade 8.

The mastery benchmarks should become the basis for the required curriculum.

Benchmarks for Continuing Development

These are benchmarks that identify processes and attitudes that are essential for all students, but should be nurtured on every appropriate occasion, rather than taught at a particular grade level. Here is a Grades 6–8 benchmark from Kendall/Marzano that would be identified as one for continuing development:

> Reflects on what has been learned after reading.
> (p. 307)

As a continuing benchmark, it would not be assigned a particular grade level but would be noted "for continuing development."

These benchmarks should be presented to teachers as reminders of the skills and attitudes they should nurture on every appropriate occasion.

Enrichment Benchmarks

These are benchmarks that are not essential for all students, but might be of interest to some. They would be taught only if the mastery benchmarks were achieved. Here is a Grades 9–12 benchmark from Kendall/Marzano that could be considered enrichment:

> Understands relatively uncommon technical terms
> used in informational texts. (p. 308)

Teachers should teach these benchmarks only if there is time and only after students mastered the mastery benchmarks.

Carrying out this analysis will reduce considerably the number of benchmarks and will aid teachers by clearly specifying what should be explicitly taught, what should be nurtured on a continuing basis, and what should be provided for enrichment.

CHECK MASTERY BENCHMARKS AGAINST HIGH-STAKES TESTS

The list of mastery benchmarks should then be checked against such high-stakes tests as state competency tests, standardized tests used by the district, and district end-of-course tests. Any concepts or skills included in such tests should, of course, be added to the mastery list.

ADD ANY NEEDED MASTERY BENCHMARKS

The final step is to add any mastery benchmarks that teachers feel are desirable. Most of the published materials, for example, do not give adequate attention to media skills and knowledge. Here is a benchmark that might be added:

Understands that television "documentaries" often include fictional elements.

PREPARE FOR CONTROVERSY

Throughout this process you should be prepared for controversy over what might be termed ideological issues. Ideologues in the field of English can be generally classified as either liberal or conservative. Those who might generally be classified as "liberal" in their view of the subject tend to advocate the following positions (see Myers, 1995, for an articulate apology for the more liberal stance):

- There are no "rights" or "wrongs" about English usage; it all depends on the context. Many so-called "correct" usages (such as "It is I") only call attention to themselves and interfere with communication.

- Children should be encouraged to use invented spelling, checking spelling correctness only for final drafts that will be seen outside the classroom.

♦ Teaching formal grammar is a waste of time and interferes with the development of more important knowledge and skills.

♦ Children should read widely among contemporary works by minority writers, giving less attention to the classics.

Those with a more conservative view of the subject challenge all these assertions. They believe that teachers should emphasize correctness in spoken and written language, stress correct spelling, teach formal grammar, and emphasize the classics. (For a reasoned defense of the more conservative position, see Zorn, 1997.)

We advocate a common sense, middle-of-the-road position.

Teachers of English language arts should clearly establish two views of language: in the eyes of linguists and anthropologists, all dialects are equal; in the eyes of gatekeepers, their dialect is the best one. In writing first drafts, students should feel free to use invented spellings, but should use spell-checkers and dictionaries to correct spelling errors in the final draft. Teaching a small number of grammatical concepts has several practical advantages: it simplifies communicating about writing; it helps the student understand the structure of the English language; and it pleases teachers of foreign languages, parents, and other citizens. And a strong literature program includes a balance of the classics and contemporary works, especially those by minority writers and women.

SUMMARY: CURRICULUM STANDARDS IN ENGLISH LANGUAGE ARTS

Figure 9.1 summarizes the status of standards in English language arts and recommends processes districts can use to develop standards-based curricula.

FIGURE 9.1. SUMMARY: CURRICULUM STANDARDS IN ENGLISH LANGUAGE ARTS

Primary sources

Kendall, J. S. & Marzano, R. J. (1996). *Content knowledge.* Aurora, CO: Mid-continent Regional Educational Laboratory.

National Council of Teaches of English & International Reading Association. (1996). *Standards for the English language arts.* Urbana, IL: Authors.

Strands used

No strands are identified in the NCTE/IRA document. Kendall/Marzano use the following: writing; reading; speaking and listening; literature; language.

Subject organization

No subject organization is specified or recommended in either report. Individual school systems often specify areas of literature study for high schools, such as this one: Grade 10, world literature; Grade 11, American literature; Grade 12, British literature.

Summary of standards

All 12 of the NCTE/IRA standards specify processes. Three of the standards focus on reading. Other standards specify the following emphases for all students: adjust language to the context; use varied writing strategies to communicate; apply knowledge of language structure and conventions; conduct research; use a variety of information sources; develop an understanding of and respect for diversity; participate in a variety of literacy communities; use language to accomplish their own purposes. One standard for students whose first language is not English specifies that they will use their first language to develop competency in the English language arts.

The standards specified in the Kendall/Marzano (1996) compilation are more balanced with respect to process and content. Kendalll and Marzano also provide grade-level benchmarks.

Recommendations to school districts

♦ Where state standards exist and are of satisfactory quality, use state standards as the foundation.

♦ Use Kendall/Marzano to add to the state standards—or to provide a foundation if state standards do not exist or lack sufficient specificity.

♦ Check the resulting product against the NCTE/IRA recommendations.

DESIGNING PERFORMANCE ASSESSMENTS

The process of designing performance assessments in English language arts is similar to the general process explained in Chapter 3. The following discussion explains how that general process would be specifically applied to English language arts.

One decision to make at the outset is to determine the extent of integration. You have three choices. *Interdisciplinary assessments* assess performance on standards from two or more subjects, such as English language arts and social studies. For example, you might decide to assess performance on these standards and their related benchmarks from Kendall and Marzano:

> ENGLISH LANGUAGE ARTS STANDARD: (Writing) Demonstrates competence in the general skills and strategies of the writing process.
>
> *Grade 6 benchmark:* Demonstrates competence in expository writing.
>
> SOCIAL STUDIES STANDARD: Understands how the early Europeans and Africans interacted with Native Americans in the Americas.

> *Grade 6 benchmark:* Understands how and why family and community life differed in various regions of colonial North America.

Here is an example of a performance assessment based on those standards and benchmarks:

> Write two personal letters. In the first, assume that you are Ben or Mabel, a young person living in colonial Pennsylvania. Write to Thomas or Abigail, your cousin living in Virginia. Explain what family and community life is like in colonial Pennsylvania. In the second letter, assume that you are Thomas or Abigail. In a letter to Ben or Mabel, explain what family and community life is like in colonial Virginia.

Subject-integrated assessments assess performance on two or more of the strands within a subject. In English language arts, this approach might integrate standards from the writing, reading, language, and literature strands. Here is an example showing how Grade 11 benchmarks from these four strands might be assessed.

> In the attached pages you will find two excerpts. The first is from Thoreau's *Walden.* The second is from Sarton's journal. Read them both carefully, focusing on the language used to respond to elements of nature. In a well-written essay that might be published in a literary journal, explain how each writer's view of nature is reflected in the language used.

Strand-focused assessments assess performance on one of the strands of English language arts. Here, for example, is a listening/speaking benchmark for Grade 6 from Kendall and Marzano: "Plays a variety of roles in group discussions..." (p. 326). Here is a strand-focused assessment based on that benchmark.

> During the final marking period, you will have an opportunity to participate in five group discus-

sions, playing one of the following roles: group leader; group recorder; active listener; chief contributor; and observer. In each instance the other members of the group will give you feedback about the effectiveness of your performance in each role.

Which of those three approaches you use will, of course, be chiefly determined by how the curriculum has been organized and delivered. In general, if students have experienced an interdisciplinary curriculum, then the assessments should be interdisciplinary.

Regardless of the final decision about integration, you should understand the nature of performance assessments in the several strands of English language arts. The following discussion uses the strands recommended above to examine the specific nature of performance assessments in each strand.

READING AND LITERATURE

To develop performance assessments in literature, you need to understand current theory on how students respond to literature. The task of classifying those responses is not a simple one. Beach and Hynds (1991) list 21 different systems for categorizing student responses to literature. One of the most widely used systems of analyzing responses is that developed by Odell and Cooper (1976). Their analysis of student responses yielded these four major categories:

- ♦ Personal (making personal statements about the reader or the work). "I was just not moved by the funeral scene."
- ♦ Descriptive (retelling the work or describing aspects of the work). "Then Harry ran off to his mother's house...."
- ♦ Interpretive (interpreting the parts or whole of the work). "I think Frost is talking mainly about the conflict between freedom and responsibility."
- ♦ Evaluative (evaluating the evocativeness, the construction, or the meaningfulness of the work). "I

just don't think she succeeded in creating realistic
characters."

The Odell-Cooper system is clear and relatively easy to
use. To make it more comprehensive from the teacher's point
of view, this author has added a fifth category:

◆ Creative (using the work as a stimulus for one's
   own creative efforts). "I think I'll write a poem
   about driving in the countryside, as an updating
   of Frost's poem."

In her excellent book on how a teacher uses writing to
teach literature, Andrasick (1990) explains how the creative
response (which she calls "imitating and transforming texts")
is a central part of her teaching of literature. Students are
asked first to imitate a text they are reading and then to trans-
form the text by using it as the basis for their own creative
writing.

The following are suggestions for using performance assessments with each of these responses.

◆ PERSONAL. Ask students to keep a journal of
   their personal responses to literature. Remind
   them that there are no right or wrong personal responses. All that matters is that the personal response be explained in depth. They can also share
   their personal responses in groups.

◆ DESCRIPTIVE. Have students write summaries
   in their journals of the works they have studied.
   The primary criterion is accuracy. As an alternative to written summaries, students can also create posters summarizing the key events of the
   plot.

◆ INTERPRETIVE. Ask students to express their
   own interpretation of the text in either verbal or
   visual forms, making specific references to the
   text itself. Current theory holds that there are no
   right or wrong interpretations of literature, only
   more reasonable and less reasonable ones. (See
   Andrasick, 1990.) If that is the stance to be taken,

then students should be encouraged to construct their own interpretations of the text, making multiple references to the text to support their interpretation.

♦ EVALUATIVE. Students should be required to evaluate a literary work. Usually the best evaluations begin with a holistic judgment of the worth of the piece, with specific criteria and ratings coming next. Evaluations can be written or oral. All evaluations should be supported by specific references to the text.

♦ CREATIVE. Students should have frequent opportunities to respond creatively to a work, using it as a motivator for their own creative writing. Their efforts should be judged on the basis of their creativity and the literary quality of the work.

Obviously, a performance assessment can combine two or more of these responses. Here is an example of a multiple-response performance task:

You are a member of a committee that has been formed to get student input into a new literature curriculum. Each committee member has been asked to recommend one current novel written for young adults. In your recommendation to the committee, deal with these issues: why the novel was important to you personally; a brief summary of the plot; your interpretation of the meaning of the novel; and your evaluation of its quality. Give special attention to your evaluation, making specific reference to the novel.

WRITING

Two issues need to be examined in using performance assessments to measure achievement in writing: how teachers should design the writing task and how students should maintain a writing portfolio.

DESIGNING THE WRITING TASKS

In the course of the school year students should be presented with at least one writing task for each of the major kinds of writing. One useful way of classifying the types of writing uses five categories: imaginative writing (creative writing, which can be related to their study of literature); expository and technical writing (explaining a process or giving directions); persuasive writing (expressing an opinion or presenting an argument); practical writing (writing as a consumer, citizen, and worker); and academic writing (using writing as a way of learning academic content). Some tasks combine two or more of these types.

Each of these writing tasks should be as authentic as possible, ones in which students write on meaningful topics for real audiences. The task should clearly indicate the topic, the type of writing, and the intended audience. Here is an example of a performance task that is primarily persuasive but that also includes some expository elements.

> The principal of your school wants students to help improve the school by identifying a problem and suggesting a solution. Write a letter to the principal in which you identify the problem, explain your solution, and tell the principal why the solution should be implemented.

MAINTAINING A WRITING PORTFOLIO

The writing portfolio is a collection of the student's writing. A review of the literature on the use and nature of the writing portfolio suggests that the best portfolios have these characteristics (see, for example, Glazer & Brown, 1993; and Murphy & Smith, 1991):

- It includes a range of writing, preferably at least one of each type.
- Its specific contents should be determined primarily by students, to give them a sense of ownership.
- It includes a piece of writing that the student considers his or her best work, with an explanation of why it is considered best.

♦ It includes a work in progress, along with an explanation of the student's plans to complete it.

♦ All entries are dated so as to show development over time.

♦ Two or more of the entries show the writing process at work, with examples of prewriting decisions, first drafts, revisions, and final versions.

♦ It includes a reflective essay in which the student considers and explains what has been learned about writing.

LANGUAGE STUDY

Language study includes these components: the structure or grammar of the language; language history; and language varieties, including dialects. Most of the performance tasks in this strand ask students to apply the knowledge they have acquired. Here are examples of the range of assessment tasks that could be used:

♦ LANGUAGE STRUCTURE. Assume that you have taken the job of tutoring a recent immigrant from one of the Central American countries. Write a "tip sheet" explaining in clear but simple language how the structure of English differs from that of Spanish.

♦ LANGUAGE HISTORY. Suppose that you have been transported to King Arthur's court. King Arthur has asked you to explain to the assembled knights how and why your language is different from theirs. What would you tell them?

♦ LANGUAGE VARIETIES. Suppose that you and your family plan to drive through rural Alabama. Your mother or your father has asked you to prepare a list reminding them of the dialect differences the family might encounter. Prepare the list that they have requested.

SPEAKING AND LISTENING

This strand also is one that will provide multiple learning experiences and assessments. Here are some of the tasks that could be used for the areas noted.

- *Interviewing.* Enable students to role play the job interview and the college interview.

- *Making formal presentations.* Have students present a speech with a specified purpose to a real or simulated audience.

- *Group discussion skills.* Train student observers to record and give feedback to group participants.

- *Listening to comprehend or follow directions.* Prepare an audio- or videotape with new information; administer a test of listening comprehension.

- *Critical listening.* Prepare a tape of a political address that makes effective use of propaganda techniques. Have students identify the specific techniques used, with examples from the speech.

MASS MEDIA AND INFORMATION PROCESSING

Although this strand is often neglected in English language arts curricula, it deals with two components that are especially needed for successful living. The chief purpose of media analysis is to develop people who can make effective and discriminating use of the mass media, especially television. Performance assessments should focus on the critical use of selected media presentations. Teachers should use videotapes of news shows, commercials, documentaries, and "soaps" that require students to exercise and demonstrate their critical judgment. Here, by way of example, is a performance task that focuses on the critical analysis of television news.

Watch closely and critically the videotape of a network news broadcast that was made last night. Take whatever notes you need to answer the following questions:

- How much time was devoted to each of the following: commercials; international news; national news; news about one state or locality; human interest features.

- How much time was devoted to each of these categories: war and violence; government and politics; celebrities in the news; weather; sports; business.

- How much time was devoted on the average to each segment or item?

Write a report summarizing your results.

Information processing includes these skills: identifying a need for information; locating and retrieving information sources; determining relevance, significance, and reliability of each source; synthesizing sources into a useful form. Most of these skills could be readily assessed in a problem-solving task that requires a broad, current, and accurate knowledge base. Here is an example of such a task:

> The legislators in our state are considering a "graduated vehicle license" program that would grant only a restricted driver's license to those ages 17–19. One of the critical issues is whether similar laws enacted in other states have been effective in reducing the number of accidents involving teenage drivers. Review the evidence on this issue. Write a letter to the legislator representing your district in which you summarize what you have learned.

USING ASSESSMENT-DRIVEN INSTRUCTION

The general instructional model presented in Chapter 4 will, for the most part, work effectively in English language arts. Modifications of it should be made, however, in teaching writing and literature.

TEACHING WRITING

The first point to be made is that teachers should develop a general approach to writing that is based upon reliable research. Figure 9.2 summarizes the key findings that should guide their approach.

FIGURE 9.2. KEY RESEARCH FINDINGS IN THE TEACHING OF WRITING

General Model

A problem-solving approach (sometimes called "the environmental mode") seems to be more effective than either the "natural process" mode (one that emphasizes journal-keeping and free-writing), the presentational mode (in which the teacher closely directs the entire writing process), and the individualized mode (in which the teacher works with one student at a time).

The Writing Curriculum

Although there is not a reliable research base with respect to curriculum models, experts generally agree that all secondary students should have instruction in and practice with several kinds of writing.

Classroom Environment

A supportive classroom environment should provide support for the writing process through an appropriate physical environment, the use of human resources, and a positive learning climate.

The Writing Process

Effective writers use the writing process flexibly, depending on the time available and the knowledge they already have.

The Writing Task

The writing assignments or tasks should be characterized by these features: they provide an opportunity for communicating about real problems to real audiences; they are broad enough to give scope for students' opinions and solutions; the tasks become increasingly

complex and challenging but are achievable with supportive instruction; they require the students to use
higher order thinking processes; they provide sufficient
guidance without overly specifying the conditions.

The quality of the writing is affected by the audience;
some evidence suggests that students write better for
their peers than for the teacher.

Effective Interventions

Teaching students a few key text structures (such as the
elements of a narrative) seems to be effective in helping
students write their own texts.

Teaching specific strategies for generating ideas, planning, and revising helps students accomplish these tasks.

Teaching students how to use sentence-combining
strategies seems to result in the writing of more mature
sentences.

Presenting students with criteria to judge their own and
their peers' writing seems to be helpful with most
students.

Emphasizing the thought processes needed in problem-
solving (such as drawing inferences, creating relationships, and abstracting large bodies of ideas) produces
better student writing.

Providing scaffolding or supportive structures (such as
cue cards, think cards, timely questions, reminders, and
timely feedback) seems to improve student writing.
The scaffolding should be reduced as students internal-
ize the strategies.

Providing ample opportunities for student-student and
student-teacher dialog seems to be a useful strategy for
both learning disabled students and non-learning–disabled; such dialogs should emphasize metacognitive
processes. Peer response groups should be used
throughout the writing process and should emphasize
peer-initiated discourse.

Ineffective Interventions

Several frequently used strategies have been shown to be ineffective in improving writing: teaching formal grammar; emphasizing mechanics; requiring students to study models of good writing; having students free-write (students write whatever comes into their minds).

Evaluation of Writing

The teacher should minimize the role of evaluator and instead provide support and constructive feedback.

Correcting students' mistakes does not seem to aid in the revision process or improve student writing.

The writing portfolio seems to be a useful means for evaluating student writing, although there are problems with reliability. Writing portfolios seem to yield the most valid results when they include multiple examples of student writing representing a variety of genres.

Revision

For high school and older students and for skilled writers, revision usually improves the final product; this is less true for younger and less skilled writers.

Providing students with a revision structure that helps them evaluate, diagnose, and revise is effective in improving the revision process. Computerized programs that prompt in this fashion seem also to be effective.

Feedback about writing from both peers and teacher improves writing for high school and older students. For high school writers, peer feedback may be more useful than teacher feedback.

(Sources: Applebee, 1984; Applebee, 1986; Cotton, 1988; Davis, 1984; Freedman et al., 1987; Hillocks, 1986; Yates, 1987.)

The second issue that needs emphasis is the importance of using a primary trait analysis in identifying the skills that need to be taught. A primary trait analysis, as the term implies, is the identification of the major characteristics that should be found in an A or B paper. You do the analysis by answering this question: "For this particular writing task and this particular group of students, what are the major features that would characterize successful performance?"

This list of traits or major features has several uses. It should guide your teaching and the kind of support you provide to students. For administrators, teachers, parents, and students, it shows how a particular strand of the writing curriculum is worked out for each grade level. It communicates clearly to students what is expected. And it provides the basis for the rubrics you use in evaluating student performance.

Figure 9.3 is an example of primary trait analysis for a Grade 7 writing task in expository writing. The list of primary traits should be kept brief; typically no more than five traits should be identified.

The teacher should teach the needed strategies before students begin to write. Those strategies may include one or more of these types: elements of the text structure (such as the standard components of argument); specific strategies for generating ideas and for planning the writing; and the thought processes required to solve the writing problem. As teachers consider this matter of teaching strategies, they should keep in mind the basic principle of scaffolding: remove the scaffolding as students gain increasing control. The results of the primary trait analysis should also be useful in deciding which strategies to teach.

One useful strategy that helps students plan is Collaborative Planning developed by Flower and colleagues (1992). In Collaborative Planning, students pair-off, with one student in each pair acting as Writer and one as Supporter. (Roles are switched so each student has a chance to play each role.) The writer explains and elaborates his or her plan to the Supporter who listens, asks questions, and encourages the writer to develop the plan. The Supporter reminds the Writer to deal with issues of content knowledge, purpose, audience, and text conventions (the distinctive features of the genre, such as

FIGURE 9.3. PRIMARY TRAIT ANALYSIS

STRAND: Exposition

GRADE: 7

WRITING TASK: Write a recipe for a favorite family food. Write the recipe so that it can be published in a class recipe book for students and their parents.

PRIMARY TRAITS

+ Identifies the food by category and by name.
+ Stimulates readers' interests in making the food.
+ Lists ingredients, with correct terms and specific measurements.
+ Gives specific directions for preparation, in chronological order.
+ Identifies family by name.

Special Notes

+ Because the recipes will be published, no errors in mechanics will be tolerated in the final draft.
+ Because the recipes are intended for a general audience, a clear simple style is preferred.

foreshadowing in the narrative). Several studies support the effectiveness of Collaborative Planning in helping students develop more effective plans and products.

+ It provides sufficient time for students to gain the knowledge they need, to plan their writing, and to complete initial drafts.
+ It provides ample time for students to work together in groups and to share their writing.
+ It provides time for students to revise. As the research summary notes, this revision will be most effective if students are provided with specific

criteria they can use in evaluating and revising their written work.

TEACHING LITERATURE

In deciding how to teach literature, teachers should know and be able to apply the research on the teaching of literature. Figure 9.4 summarizes the major findings that have relevance for teaching. Teachers should reflect about the research as it relates to what they have learned experientially by being both a reader and a teacher of literature.

How teachers apply these research-based strategies will depend upon several factors: teachers' preferred teaching style; teachers' and students' strengths and needs; the literary work; the time available; and the purpose for teaching that work. The following general model integrates several of these research-based strategies and reflects the experience of expert teachers. (See Young, 1986; Andrasick, 1990; and Squire, 1995.)

- ◆ PREREADING. Present the work in a manner that will elicit students' motivation to read it; however, avoid overpraising the work. Also spend some time activating their prior knowledge about the author and the work. Here is an example of an effective presentation:

    The Red Badge of Courage is a novel that will give you a deeper understanding of the nature of courage. It will also give you a true picture of the nature of war as it used to be. What do you think "the red badge of courage" might be? What do you know about the Civil War?

- ◆ ENCOUNTER WITH THE WHOLE WORK. Provide time for the students to read the entire work independently. Andrasick notes that in her teaching she tries to replicate the way people actually read novels by requiring the students to read the entire work before class discussion. The "chapter-at-a-time" approach that many teachers use distorts the nature of the reading experience and results in a fragmented understanding. Instead,

FIGURE 9.4. RESEARCH IN THE EFFECTIVE TEACHING OF LITERATURE

The research in general suggests that the following practices are likely to result in more positive attitudes towards literature and more insightful readings of literary texts.

Selection of Materials

Select and make available diversified materials that students can read, that appeal to students, and that make connections with their own lives.

General Predispositions

Develop in students an attitude of openness about literature. Remind them that they should suspend disbelief as they encounter a new work and begin with a positive attitude towards the characters in the work.

Discussion Strategies

Ask authentic, open-ended questions that help students reflect about and understand their responses to literature.

Ask questions that help students relate the work to their own experience.

Use student answers in advancing the discussion.

Do not rush the discussion; take time to let students explore through talking and listening.

Provide frequent opportunities for students to talk together about what they have read independently.

Writing about Literature

Require students to write longer pieces stating and explaining their response to the work. Avoid short-answer exercises for both in-class and homework assignments.

Group Structures

Use student-led small group discussions frequently as a means of encouraging students to speak openly about their response to literature.

Curriculum

Structure the literature curriculum so that it is coherent, enabling students to make connections between literary works and to examine issues on a continuing basis.

(Sources: Beach & Hynds, 1991; Martinez & Roser, 1991; Nystrand, 1990; Applebee, Burroughs, & Stevens, 1994; Squire, 1995.)

Andrasick gives students copies of the work a few weeks in advance of the time designated for discussing it. Students are expected to have read the entire book when they come to class on that first day of discussion.

Thus, students would receive copies of *The Red Badge of Courage* perhaps two weeks in advance of the time for class discussion.

♦ INDIVIDUAL RESPONSES: PERSONAL AND DESCRIPTIVE. Have students write in their journals two brief responses. First, they should write a personal response, explaining their personal reaction to the work. Then they should write a descriptive response, summarizing the key elements of the work to show that they have read it. A brief quiz can also be used to determine if students have read the work with sufficient comprehension to be able to discuss it. These two responses should be made without discussion, so that individual readers are not influenced by the reactions of peers.

Here is an example of a personal response that a student might make to *The Red Badge of Courage:*

For some reason I just didn't connect with this novel. I think it seemed too old-fashioned for me. I think I'm addicted to computer games of futuristic conflict.

◆ SMALL-GROUP DISCUSSION. A student-led small-group discussion ensues, in which students check their comprehension and share with each other their personal responses. Prior to this, they should have received training on how to respond to someone else's personal response. Each group reports briefly on the tenor of their discussion.

Here is an example of a group report.

Most of our group started with negative feelings about this novel. However, all of us, except one person, were able to identify with the main characters.

◆ DEEPER UNDERSTANDING. The teacher decides which response to elicit next—the interpretive or the evaluative. For both responses the students write in their journals, without discussion. They then share their responses in a student-led discussion. Each group makes a brief report.

An alternative strategy here is to use cooperative inquiry. Each small group would be responsible for investigating in depth one aspect of the work. For example, the teacher might set up these inquiry groups for *The Red Badge of Courage*:

- Character development in the novel.
- Imagery in the novel.
- The novel as an example of Naturalism.
- The theme of the novel.

◆ GUIDED DISCUSSION. For either response the teacher now plays a more active and guiding role in a whole-class discussion, building upon the results of the small-group talk.

Here are some questions that a teacher might pose in a guided class discussion of imagery in *The Red Badge of Courage.*

- Let us list all the references to nature in the novel.
- How do elements of nature influence events in the plot?
- In what sense do elements of nature affect the characters?
- What view of nature does Crane hold, as you understand the novel?

◆ REFLECTIVE RESPONSE. After the class discussion each student then writes a reflective response that integrates what the student has learned from prior responses, from the group discussion, and from the whole-class analysis.

Here is part of a student's reflective response, after having been engaged in all the above activities:

> As I noted in my journal entry, I first read the book as a simple war story. And I found myself being put off by references to old-fashioned things. Now I find myself thinking about the meaning of courage....

◆ CREATIVE RESPONSE. With selected works the students imitate the style or use the work as a stimulus for their own creativity.

In the example above, the teacher might decide to conclude the unit by having students write a personal narrative telling about one time when their own courage was tested.

The above model is presented here as a set of flexible guidelines, which teachers should evaluate, modify, test in a classroom setting, and extend to suit the teacher's instructional purposes. Literature should not be taught with a rigid formula.

REFERENCES

Andrasick, K.D. (1990). *Opening texts: Using writing to teach literature.* Portsmouth, NH: Heinemann.

Applebee, A.N. (1984). *Contexts for learning to write.* Norwood, NJ: Ablex.

Applebee, A.N. (1986). Problems in process approaches: Toward a reconceptualization of process instruction. In A.R. Petrosky & D. Bartholomae (Eds.), *The teaching of writing* (pp. 95–113). Chicago: University of Chicago Press.

Applebee, A.N., Burroughs, R., & Stevens, A.S. (1994). *Shaping conversations: A study of continuity and coherence in high school literature curricula.* Albany, NY: National Research Center on English Learning and Achievement, State University of New York at Albany.

Beach, R., & Hynds, S. (1991). Research on response to literature. In R. Barr, M.L. Kamil, P.B. Mosenthal, & P.D. Pearson, *Handbook of reading research, volume II* (pp. 453–489). New York: Longman.

Brewbaker, J.M. (1997). On Tuesday morning: The case for standards for the English language arts. *English Journal, 86* (1), 76–82.

Cotton, K. (1988). *Teaching composition: Research on effective practices.* Portland, OR: Northwest Regional Educational Laboratory.

Davis, D.J. (1984). *Writing across the curriculum: A research review.* ERIC Document Reproduction Service No. ED 254 848.

Flower, L., Norris, L., Wallace, D., & Burnett, R. (1992). *Making thinking visible: A collaborative look at collaborative planning.* Urbana, IL: National Council of Teachers of English.

Freedman, S.W., Dyson, A.H., Flower, L., & Chafe, W. (1987). *Research in writing: Past, present, and future.* Berkeley, CA: Center for the Study of Writing, University of California Berkeley.

Glatthorn, A.A. (1994). *Developing the quality curriculum.* Alexandria, VA: Association for Supervision and Curriculum Development.

Glatthorn, A.A. (1995). A mastery curriculum for English language arts. In A.A. Glatthorn (Ed.), *Content of the curriculum* (2d ed.) (pp. 61–68). Alexandria, VA: Association for Supervision and Curriculum Development.

Glazer, S.M., & Brown, C.S. (1993). *Portfolios and beyond: Collaborative assessment in reading and writing.* Norwood, MA: Christopher-Gordon.

Hillocks, G., Jr. (1986). *Research on written composition: New directions for teaching.* Urbana, IL: National Conference on Research in English.

Kendall, J.S., & Marzano, R.J. (1996). *Content knowledge.* Aurora, CO: Mid-continent Regional Educational Laboratory.

Maloney, H.B. (1997). The little standards that couldn't. *English Journal, 86* (1).

Martinez, M.G., & Roser, N.L. (1991). Children's responses to literature. In J. Flood, J.M. Jensen, D. Lapp, & J.R. Squire (Eds.), *Handbook of research on teaching the English language arts* (pp. 643–654). New York: Macmillan.

Murphy, S., & Smith, M.A. (1991). *Writing portfolios: A bridge from teaching to assessment.* Markham, ON: Pippin.

Myers, M. (1995). English language arts: Public-professional tensions in the standards debate. In A.A. Glatthorn (Ed.), *Content of the curriculum* (2nd ed.) (pp. 23–60). Alexandria, VA: Association for Supervision and Curriculum Development.

Myers, M., & Spalding (Eds.). (1997). *Exemplar series, grades 6–8.* Urbana, IL: National Council of Teachers of English.

National Council of Teachers of English & International Reading Association. (1996). *Standards for the English language arts.* Urbana, IL: Author.

Nystrand, M. (1990). *Making it hard: Curriculum and instruction as factors in difficulty of literature.* Albany, NY: Center for the Learning and Teaching of Literature, State University of New York at Albany.

Odell, L., & Cooper, C. (1976). Describing responses to works of fiction. *Research in the Teaching of English, 10,* 203–225.

Smagorinsky, P. (1996). *Standards in practice: Grades 9–12.* Urbana, IL: National Council of Teachers of English.

Speech Communication Association. (1996). *Speaking, listening, and media literacy standards for K through 12 education.* Annandale, VA: Author.

Squire, J.R. (1995). Language arts. In G. Cawelti (Ed.), *Handbook of research on improving student achievement* (pp. 71–86). Arlington, VA: Educational Research Service.

Yates, J.M. (1987). *Research implications for writing in the content areas: What research says to the teacher* (2nd ed.). Washington, DC: National Education Association.

Young, A.E. (1986). Fostering response to literature in the college English classroom. (Doctoral dissertation, University of Pennsylvania.) *Dissertation Abstracts International, 47,* 1268A.

Zorn, J. (1997). The NCTE/IRA Standards: A surrender. *English Journal, 86* (1), 83–85.

10

IMPLEMENTING THE ACHIEVEMENT CYCLE

Implementing a complex project such as the achievement cycle requires effective leadership and careful planning. This concluding chapter examines this complexity by suggesting a general strategy and then offering some specific suggestions about each phase of implementation.

USING A GENERAL IMPLEMENTATION STRATEGY

The project should be conceived as one major change (the achievement cycle) that involves three closely related components (curriculum, assessment, and instruction) that are all focused on the ultimate goal of improving authentic learning.

ENSURE THAT THE ORGANIZATIONAL STRUCTURES ARE IN PLACE

As explained in Chapter 1, the project requires several organizational structures—or their equivalent committees. The Project Planning Council is responsible for planning and monitoring the entire district project. A Citizens Advisory Council provides input to the school board. The planning council appoints Subject Task Forces as needed; each task force is responsible for the project as it involves one subject such as science. Most task forces will work with a K-12 responsibility, although some districts may decide to use school-level task forces, such as middle school or high school. At the school level a School Coordinating Council (or the school improvement committee) coordinates all the school-based activities. The instructional teams do the specific work required for change at the classroom level.

DEVELOP A RESEARCH-BASED CHANGE STRATEGY

The planning council should articulate and implement a change strategy based on sound research. Figure 10.1 summarizes the key findings that can guide implementers. While the research guidelines suggest some useful recommendations to keep in mind, they should be viewed flexibly, because the local context will obviously have an impact.

FIGURE 10.1. SUMMARY OF RESEARCH: IMPLEMENTATION OF CHANGE

- ◆ Ensure that a supportive culture is in place—one that embodies the values of collegiality, inquiry, and continuous improvement.
- ◆ Develop a vision of what you hope to accomplish, but revisit the vision as you act and learn. The best change strategy is an evolutionary process that uses current data and builds consensus to guide direction and action.
- ◆ Clarify the goals of the project so that everyone involved understands where the project is headed.
- ◆ Develop strong support at the superintendent and central office levels while ensuring collegial decision-making; a combined top-down, bottom-up strategy seems to work best.
- ◆ Provide continuing training for teachers, reinforcing the skills with peer coaching.
- ◆ Strengthen leadership at all levels; specify the needed leadership functions and ensure that they are being discharged. Avoid relying solely on the principal.
- ◆ Ensure that needed resources are available in a timely manner.
- ◆ Ensure that change is systemic, so that program components reinforce and sustain each other.

Sources: Corbett & Wilson, 1992; Fullan, 1992; Hord, 1996; Stringfield, 1996; Stringfield & Teddlie, 1988.

TRAIN THE PROJECT PLANNING COUNCIL

Once the planning council has been appointed, training should be provided, either by an external consultant, a representative from the educational service or regional center, or an internal administrator or supervisor who has had special training. The trainer should provide workshops dealing with these topics.

+ Understanding the achievement cycle.
+ Broadening the knowledge base: the research on implementation.
+ Broadening the knowledge base: the research on the achievement cycle.
+ The nature and importance of authentic learning.
+ Developing standards-based curricula.
+ Developing performance assessments.
+ Fostering assessment-driven instruction

This training should emphasize the development of awareness and basic knowledge; it can be supplemented as needed when major phases of the project are ready for development.

ORIENT ALL THOSE INVOLVED

With the basic training completed, the planning council should then provide a general orientation to the school board, central office supervisors, school administrators, and teacher-leaders. At this stage, according to the Stages of Concern research, participants will only have general concerns about the nature of the project. (See Hord, Rutherford, Huling-Austin, & Hall, 1987, for the research on "stages of concern.") The orientation should ensure that all participants have a clear understanding of the project's vision and goals.

DEVELOP A FLEXIBLE LONG-TERM PLANNING CALENDAR

The planning council should develop a flexible long-term planning calendar. An example is shown in Figure 10.2 on the next page. First, priorities are established after a needs assess-

FIGURE 10.2. GENERAL PLANNING CALENDAR

SUBJ/YEAR	01–02	02–03	03–04	04–05	05–06
ARTS		Curriculum	Assessment	Instruction	
ENG LANG ARTS	Curriculum	Curriculum	Assessment	Assessment	Instruction
FOREIGN LANG			Curriculum	Assessment	Assessment
MATH	Curriculum	Assessment	Assessment	Instruction	Instruction
SCIENCE		Curriculum	Curriculum	Assessment	Assessment
SOCIAL STUDIES				Curriculum	Curriculum
VOCATIONAL					Curriculum

ment that considers such factors as the number of students affected, the present state of curriculum, assessment, and instruction in the subjects, and the readiness of the faculty. Then, for each subject a determination is made of the number of years required for developing curricula, producing performance assessments, and helping teachers develop and implement assessment-based units. In some cases, each of these phases can be accomplished in one year; in other instances, two years will be needed. This determination is based on the complexity of the task and the resources available. Then the three phases are entered for each subject, considering the resources available and the ability of the teachers to handle change.

PROVIDE INTENSIVE TRAINING FOR SCHOOL ADMINISTRATORS

Even with overall district planning and direction, the school principal still plays a critical role if the program is to be successfully implemented. These topics should be considered in developing an agenda for administrator training.

- ♦ Understanding the nature and importance of the achievement cycle.
- ♦ Orienting teachers to the entire project and eliciting their support.
- ♦ Working with parents to support the project.
- ♦ Providing leadership in curriculum.
- ♦ Providing leadership in performance assessment.
- ♦ Providing leadership in assessment-driven instruction.
- ♦ Sharing leadership with teachers.
- ♦ Monitoring project progress and identifying problems.

APPOINT, TRAIN, AND MONITOR THE WORK OF TASK FORCES

The planning council is also responsible for appointing the task forces needed for each phase of the project. As indicated previously, we recommend subject-focused task forces. Larger districts may decide to have three task forces for each subject; thus, there would be a Math Curriculum Task Force, a Math Performance Assessment Task Force, and a Math Assessment-Driven Instruction Task Force. In smaller districts, one task force for each subject would do the work for all three phases.

Task force members need to have the training necessary to function effectively in their roles. Such training, of course, should be project-specific, delivered immediately prior to need. The planning council should also monitor the work of each task force, requesting plans, checking progress reports, and evaluating the products.

IMPLEMENTING CURRICULUM DEVELOPMENT

The implementation of the curriculum project will be effective if leaders keep in mind the factors affecting successful implementation identified earlier. In addition to the general strategy previously explicated, the curriculum task forces should keep in mind the special planning approaches required for quality curriculum work.

DETERMINE SCOPE OF CURRICULUM DEVELOPMENT

The first job of the Project Planning Council in its curriculum work is to determine the scope of the curriculum project by first determining what subjects will be included and then deciding which grade levels will be covered. The answers will be determined by analyzing the resources available and assessing needs. However, two general recommendations can be made. First, include all subjects in standards-based curriculum development. An excellent program of studies requires quality in all fields. (Limitations of length required this book to focus on the four academic subjects.) Second, include all grades, because a well-coordinated K-12 curriculum is more effective than a fragmented collection of pieces.

IDENTIFY PRIORITIES

The next task is for the planning council to determine which subjects will be given the highest priority in the development process. These questions can guide this decision-making.

+ When were curriculum guides last revised? (Older guides receive higher priority.)

+ How many students take each subject? (Subjects with high enrollments receive higher priority.)

+ How much have the subjects changed in recent years? (Greater changes warrant a higher priority.)

+ When were textbooks last purchased? (Subjects with older texts receive higher priority.)

+ What do supervisors, teachers, and school administrators recommend? (Their recommendations should be given the greatest weight.)

The planning council should use these decisions about scope and priorities in developing a curriculum planning calendar, similar to the one shown in Figure 10.3 on the next page; this curriculum planning calendar will supplement the general project calendar explained earlier. Note that the calendar identifies for each subject four phases of the development process. In the PLAN phase, the subject task force builds its knowledge base, develops its own detailed calendar, secures the needed resources, and acquires the skills they need.

In the PRODUCE phase, the task force accomplishes the specific steps explained in Chapter 2. In the PILOT phase, the task force arranges to have the materials pilot tested in selected schools. In the IMPLEMENT phase, the revised materials are implemented throughout the district. (For additional details see Glatthorn, 1994.) A five-year calendar, periodically revised, is recommended. (Note that the figure includes only four years and four subjects, as a means of conserving space.)

Once the planning calendar has been approved, the planning council should appoint the subject task forces as needed. The subject task forces are then responsible for the steps explained in the following sections.

FIGURE 10.3. CURRICULUM DEVELOPMENT CALENDAR

YEAR/ SUBJECT	01–02	02–03	03–04	04–05
ARTS		Plan Produce	Pilot Implement	
FOREIGN LANGUAGE		Plan	Produce	Pilot
MATHEMATICS	Plan	Produce	Pilot	Implement
READING/ LANGUAGE ARTS				Plan

DEVELOP SUBJECT-SPECIFIC PLANNING CALENDAR

The subject task force should develop its own detailed planning calendar, using the steps identified in Chapter 2. Their proposed calendar should be reviewed by the Project Planning Council.

PROVIDE TRAINING FOR TEACHERS INVOLVED

As explained in Chapter 2, teachers should be actively involved throughout the curriculum development process. Their input is needed for several of the steps: identifying priorities among the standards; reviewing content decisions; identifying and reviewing benchmarks; analyzing benchmarks into learning objectives. Their input can be most useful only if it is based upon a current and sound knowledge base. As a consequence, their training might include the following. (Mathematics is used as an example.)

- The nature of mathematics standards.
- Essential and enrichment standards.
- Standards for continuing development.
- Benchmarks and their nature.

- Cognitive development and benchmark placement.
- The mathematics curriculum guide.
- Learning objectives in mathematics

EVALUATE AND REVISE

With the guidance of the planning council, the subject task force should perform and arrange for several forms of formative and summative evaluation. First, they should evaluate their own work as it progresses. Second, they should secure reviews from supervisors, administrators, and teachers as the products are completed. They should also arrange for and supervise the piloting of the materials in several schools and grades. Finally, they should secure an external review by experts in the field. They should use the results of these assessments to improve the quality of their work.

PROVIDE FOR CURRICULUM ALIGNMENT AND MONITORING

The implementation will be more effective if the curriculum groups ensure that the written curriculum is aligned with the performance assessments and the learning resources. They should also work with principals in developing a curriculum monitoring system that ensures the curriculum is being implemented with reasonable fidelity.

IMPLEMENTING PERFORMANCE ASSESSMENTS

If performance assessments have been developed, tested, and revised, then the two major tasks for the implementation stage are to ensure that they are being used and to evaluate their effectiveness and overall quality. To accomplish the first goal, the principal needs to play a key role. Principals should ask teachers to submit a tentative calendar showing when they plan to use the special assessments. They should review the plan in dialog with the teachers, examining the number to be used and the frequency of use.

That plan can then guide the principal in making classroom observations. Those observations can serve three purposes: They indicate the principal's interest in the project;

they serve as a reminder to the teachers that they are expected to use the assessments; and they enable the principal to gather formative data about the quality of the assessments.

The quality can also be assessed by classroom teachers as they use the performance tasks. They should focus on such questions as the following.

- How much class time did they require?
- What problems did students experience?
- What instructional problems did they seem to cause?
- What results did students achieve?

IMPLEMENTING ASSESSMENT-DRIVEN INSTRUCTION

Implementing assessment driven instruction effectively is probably the most challenging task of all. Teachers have deeply ingrained teaching styles and rely to a great extent on what has worked in the past. However, with the right kind of training and support, they can acquire the newer skills required for assessment driven instruction.

The training is crucial. It should be an ongoing process that gives teachers the skills they need before they need them—and reinforces those skills periodically as needed. The workshops should be supplemented with peer coaching that enables teachers to give colleagues objective feedback and coach each other on skill acquisition and use. The following topics provide a useful focus for the staff development:

- Understanding assessment-driven instruction.
- Developing assessment-based units.
- Implementing assessment-based units.
- Understanding current models of teaching and their relation to assessment-driven instruction.
- Maintaining a focus on performance assessments.
- Monitoring student learning.
- Coaching for mastery of assessment-driven instruction.

The structure of the workshops and the teaching/learning processes used should reflect the best current knowledge about effective staff development programs. Figure 10.4 summarizes that research.

FIGURE 10.4. SUMMARY OF RESEARCH: STAFF DEVELOPMENT

The research on staff development and organizational change suggests that these recommendations should be implemented in designing and delivering staff development:

Structure

♦ Ensure that there is a culture in place that supports development, collaboration, and inquiry.

♦ Provide the staff development for the entire organization, not just for small groups.

♦ Develop and implement a coherent plan that provides for systemic change.

♦ Provide adequate quality time for staff development, offered on a long-term basis.

Content

♦ Focus on student learning; ensure that all components address student achievement.

♦ Emphasize job-embedded learning, providing for reflection on real-world experiences.

♦ Focus on curriculum, instruction, and technology.

♦ Provide for both generic and subject-specific content.

Strategies

♦ Use instructional strategies that reflect models of effective teaching.

♦ Support the staff development workshops with peer coaching.

♦ Emphasize the analysis of and reflection about classroom data and experiences.

(Sources: Filby, 1995; Joyce & Showers, 1995; Sparks, 1995; Sparks & Hirsh, 1997.)

A CONCLUDING NOTE

Implementing the achievement cycle requires skilled leadership, committed followership, and adequate resources. However, the result is better learning for all.

REFERENCES

Corbett, H.D., & Wilson, B. (1992). The central office role in instructional improvement. *School effectiveness and School Improvement, 3* (1), 45–68.

Filby, N.N. (1995). *Analysis of reflective professional development models.* San Francisco: WestEd.

Fullan, M.G. (1992). Overcoming barriers to educational change. In *Changing schools: Insights* (pp. 11–20). Washington, DC: U.S. Department of Education.

Hord, S. (1996). Realizing school improvement through understanding the change process. In R.E. Blum & J.A. Arter (Eds.), *Student performance assessment in an era of restructuring,* pp. VIII-10:1–5. Alexandria, VA: Association for Supervision and Curriculum Development.

Hord, S.M., Rutherford, W.L., Huling-Austin, L., & Hall, G.E. (1987). *Taking charge of change.* Alexandria, VA: Association for Supervision and Curriculum Development.

Joyce, B., & Showers, B. (1995). *Student achievement through staff development* (2d ed.). New York: Longman.

Sparks, D. (1995). Focusing staff development on student learning. In G. Cawelti (Ed.), *Handbook of research on improving student achievement* (pp. 163–169). Arlington, VA: Educational Research Service.

Sparks, D., & Hirsh, S. (1997). *A new vision for staff development.* Alexandria, VA: Association for Supervision and Curriculum Development.

Stringfield, S. (1996). Attempting to enhance students' learning. In R.E. Blum & J.A. Arter (Eds.), *Student performance assessment in an era of restructuring,*pp. VIII-2:1–6. Alexandria, VA: Association for Supervision and Curriculum Development.

Stringfield, S., & Teddlie, C. (1988). A time to summarize: The Louisiana effectiveness study. *Educational Leadership, 46* (2), 43–49.